PEACE WITH CHINA?
U.S. DECISIONS FOR ASIA

Edited by Earl C. Ravenal

WITH CONTRIBUTIONS BY

JOHN W. DOWER	ROBERT E. OSGOOD
DANIEL ELLSBERG	MARCUS G. RASKIN
RICHARD A. FALK	EARL C. RAVENAL
LESLIE H. GELB	LEONARD RODBERG
MORTON H. HALPERIN	FRANZ SCHURMANN
STANLEY M. KANAROWSKI	CHARLES P. SHIRKEY
RICHARD F. KAUFMAN	LEON SLOSS
MILTON KOTLER	PIERRE M. SPREY
SEYMOUR MELMAN	WILLIAM W. WHITSON

INSTITUTE FOR POLICY STUDIES
WASHINGTON, D.C.

LIVERIGHT | NEW YORK

LIVERIGHT

Earl C. Ravenal's remarks, "The Nixon Doctrine, Defense Policy, and China," were published, in an altered version, in *Foreign Affairs,* January 1971.

John W. Dower's remarks, "The Hidden Significance of the Nixon Doctrine," appeared in a revised version as Chapter 32 of *The Indochina Story,* edited by the Committee of Concerned Asian Scholars (New York: Bantam Books, 1970). A greatly expanded version appears in *The Bulletin of Concerned Asian Scholars,* Fall 1970.

Daniel Elsberg's remarks, "Politics, Intervention, and Escalation," derive from a paper, "Escalating in a Quagmire," presented at the American Political Science Association Convention, September, 1970. An abridged version, "The Quagmire Myth and the Stalemate Machine," appeared in *Public Policy,* May 1971.

William W. Whitson's remarks, "The Chinese Threat and the Problem of Deterrence," derive from a paper, "Organizational Perspectives and Decision-making in the Chinese Communist High Command," presented at the Conference on Chinese Communist Elites at Banff, Canada, July 1970.

Earl C. Ravenal's Epilogue, "Beyond 1972—The Political-Military Gap," was published, in an altered version, in *Foreign Policy,* Summer 1971.

All sections are presented here by permission of the authors and publishers.

1.987654321

International Standard Book Number: 0-87140-545-8 (cloth)
0-87140-061-8 (paper)
Library of Congress Catalog Card Number: 71-162433

Designed by Charlotte Thorp
Manufactured in the United States of America

CONTENTS

Contributors

JOHN W. DOWER. Assistant Professor of History, University of Wisconsin; Associate Editor: *Bulletin of Concerned Asian Scholars*. Co-author and Editor: *The Indochina Story*.

DANIEL ELLSBERG. Senior Research Associate, Center for International Studies, Massachusetts Institute of Technology; former Consultant, RAND Corporation, on politics and pacification in Vietnam, 1967-1970; Special Assistant to Assistant Secretary of Defense (International Security Affairs), 1964-1965; member of Major General Lansdale's Senior Liaison Office, Saigon, 1965-1966; Special Assistant to Deputy Ambassador Porter, 1966.

RICHARD A. FALK. Albert G. Millbank Professor of International Law and Practice, Princeton University; former Counsel to Senate Committee on Foreign Relations and U. S. Arms Control and Disarmament Agency; Counsel before the International Court of Justice. Author: *Law, War, and Morality in the Contemporary World*. Editor: *The Strategy of World Order* and *The Vietnam War and International Law*. Co-editor: *The Future of the International Legal Order*.

LESLIE H. GELB. Senior Fellow, Brookings Institution; Consultant, RAND Corporation; former Acting Deputy Assistant Secretary of Defense for Policy Planning and Arms Control, 1969; Acting Director, Policy Planning Staff, Office of Assistant Secretary of Defense (International Security Affairs), 1968; Chairman, Office of the Secretary of Defense Vietnam

Task Force, 1967-1968; Executive Assistant to Senator Javits, 1966-1967; Assistant Professor of Government, Wesleyan University, 1964-1966.

MORTON H. HALPERIN. Senior Fellow, Brookings Institution; former Senior Staff Member, National Security Council, 1969; Deputy Assistant Secretary of Defense for Policy Planning and Arms Control, 1966-1968; Assistant Professor of Government, Harvard University, 1964-1966; Research Associate, Harvard Center for International Affairs, 1960-1966. Author: *Contemporary Military Strategy; China and the Bomb; Limited War in the Nuclear Age.* Co-author: *Strategy and Arms Control; Communist China and Arms Control.*

STANLEY M. KANAROWSKI. Major, U. S. Army; Special Assistant to the Deputy Commanding General, Army Combat Development Command; former Staff Member, National Security Council, 1969-1970; Staff Member, Office of the Assistant Secretary of Defense (Systems Analysis), 1966-1969; Coordinator, Interagency Program Analysis of Korea, 1968-1969; Staff Officer, Headquarters MACV and 1st Infantry Division, Vietnam, 1965-1966.

RICHARD F. KAUFMAN. Staff Economist and Counsel, Joint Economic Committee of the U. S. Congress. Author: *The War Profiteers.*

MILTON KOTLER. Resident Fellow, Institute for Policy Studies; Contributing Editor: *Ramparts,* Author: *Neighborhood Government.*

SEYMOUR MELMAN. Professor of Industrial Engineering, Columbia University; Consultant to industrial management and Government. Author: *Pentagon Capitalism: The Political Economy of War; Our Depleted Society; The Peace Race; Decision-Making and Productivity; Dynamic Factors in Productivity.* Editor: *Conversion of Industry from a Military to Civilian Economy; Inspection for Disarmament.*

ROBERT E. OSGOOD. Professor of American Foreign Policy, The Johns Hopkins School of Advanced International Studies; Director, Washington Center of Foreign Policy Research; former

Senior Staff Member, National Security Council, 1969-1970; Professor of Political Science, University of Chicago, 1956-1961. Author: *Alliances and American Foreign Policy, NATO: The Entangling Alliance; Limited War: The Challenge to American Strategy; Ideals and Self-Interest in America's Foreign Relations.* Co-author: *America and the World; Japan and the United States in Asia; Force, Order and Justice.*

MARCUS G. RASKIN. Co-Director, Institute for Policy Studies; Associate Editor: *Ramparts;* former Education Advisor, Office of the President, 1963; Member, U. S. Disarmament Delegation at Geneva, 1963; Staff Member, National Security Council, 1961-1962; Legislative Counsel to twelve Democratic Congressmen, 1958-1961; Staff Editor, *The Liberal Papers,* 1961. Author: *Being and Doing.* Co-author: *New American Manifesto; After Twenty Years: Alternatives to the Cold War in Europe; Deterrence and Reality.* Co-editor: *Viet-Nam Reader.*

EARL C. RAVENAL. Associate Fellow, Institute for Policy Studies; former Director, Asian Division (Systems Analysis), Office of the Secretary of Defense, 1967-1969; Director, Interagency Program Analysis of Korea, 1968-1969; author of Secretary of Defense Memorandum to the President on Asian Strategy and Force Structure.

LEONARD RODBERG. Visiting Fellow, Institute for Policy Studies; former Professor of Physics, University of Maryland, 1966-1970; Chief of Policy Research for Science and Technology, U. S. Arms Control and Disarmament Agency, 1961-1966. Author: *Quantum Theory of Scattering.* Editor: *The Pentagon Watchers.*

FRANZ SCHURMANN. Professor of Sociology and History, University of California, Berkeley; Director, Bay Area Institute. Author: *Ideology and Organization in Communist China.*

CHARLES P. SHIRKEY. Research Associate, Brookings Institution; Consultant to Under Secretary of State; former Staff Member, Office of the Assistant Secretary of Defense (Systems Analysis), 1968-1970; Budget Examiner, National Security Programs, Bureau of the Budget, 1965-1968.

LEON SLOSS.   Director, Combined Policy, Office of Political-Military Affairs, Department of State; former Assistant Director, Strategic Studies Center, Stanford Research Institute, 1960-1965; Vice President, Conlon Associates, Ltd., management consultants specializing in Asia, 1958-1960. Author of several articles on Asian and strategic policy.

PIERRE M. SPREY.   Manager, Systems Division, Enviro Control, Inc.; former Special Assistant to the Assistant Secretary of Defense (Systems Analysis) and Staff Member, 1965-1970; Research Scientist and Engineer, Grumman Aircraft Corporation, 1958-1965.

WILLIAM W. WHITSON.   Staff Member, RAND Corporation; former Colonel, U. S. Army; Special Assistant to Deputy Assistant Secretary of Defense (Systems Analysis), 1969-1970; U. S. Army Intelligence assignments, Taiwan and Hong Kong, 1963-1969. Author: *The Chinese Communist High Command: A History of Military Politics, 1927-69.*

I

INTRODUCTION
by EARL C. RAVENAL

EARL C. RAVENAL

Policy, Prophecy,
and National Action

After a quarter-century of impassive hostility, almost suddenly there is the prospect of vast change in America's relationship with China and all of Asia. The Ping-Pong diplomacy of the spring of 1971 and the Nixon administration's openings toward China excited expectations as well as speculations. Can the United States government—beset by pressures and hedged by constraints—fulfill the hopes that have been aroused?

For what appears to be news—that American intentions toward China seem now to be benign—is not really surprising. Governments *intend,* if they can, to meet their objectives and promote their interests through peace rather than conflict. And they would be more than content to accomplish their purposes simply and totally, even if these purposes are incompatible with the stubborn objective features of the situation.

That much is not novel; it is not even empirically interesting—it could be established a priori. More important are the contradictions: our government signals an accommodation with China but works for a regime of "stability" in Asia; it promotes its continuing influence around China's periphery but seeks China's acquiescence in this scheme; it insists on its alliances with China's political enemies and ideological antagonists but advertises, through the Nixon Doctrine, that it will be free of the consequences of involvement in Asia; it pursues constructive contact with China, without constructive concessions. In short, it seeks peace with China, without facing the ultimate American decisions for Asia.

Unfortunately, in these neat antitheses there is more than irony; there are the seeds of continuing tension and periodic conflict. Self-contradictory policies lead to present illusion and future frustration and danger. All the more reason now to look at the U. S. relationship with China and Asia structurally and unwishfully, probing for the systemic and attitudinal factors in American government, politics, society, and economy that condition our nation's behavior in the world.

This book is inspired by a conference held at the Institute for Policy Studies in Washington, D. C. during September 1970. A group of eighteen scholars, present and former government officials, and specialists in Asia or the national security process met to discuss their experience and insights. This was one of the earliest critiques of the Nixon Doctrine and its implications for America's relations with China and its strategy in Asia. The Doctrine was just beginning to take shape through administration statements and attempted applications to various tangible U. S. actions in the world—particularly in Asia, where the Doctrine was first announced, and to which it was to be principally applied.

But the conference did not simply criticize a doctrine. It also examined the logic of our foreign policy toward Asia. And this required not only a weighing of U. S. substantive options, but an examination of the policy *process*—the institutions, the decision-making mechanisms, the pressures and compulsions, the incentives and motivations. It was an attempt, among other things, to make sense of the policy process—even where sometimes sense could not be made of the policies themselves. It looked at policy formation, not as the day-to-day existentialism of the office-holder and the decision-maker, but rather as a logical and philosophical process, and also as a technical and systematic process. It sought to bring together the related issues that go toward the production of U. S. strategy in Asia; to elucidate the causal connections among a number of otherwise very diverse elements.

In another dimension, it brought together a range of contributions that is unusually broad—though no attempt was made either to fabricate an adversary proceeding or to shape a consensus. The contributors assembled not as ideologues but as scholars and practitioners whose thought and action are influenced and moved by logic and analysis.

The book begins with an explication of the Nixon Doctrine. My paper, "The Nixon Doctrine, Defense Policy, and China," provides a broader context for consideration of the Doctrine by relating it to our military policy and preparations. It restates the political-military choices available to the U. S. in its posture toward China. It specifies the conditions for an accommodation with China and suggests the logical and historical inevitability of such a resolution.

Leslie Gelb follows with a frank questioning of the unresolved multiple meanings of the Nixon Doctrine: whether it is (1) a straightforward policy of Asian self-reliance, amounting fundamentally to force substitution; (2) a return toward massive retaliation and a more remote application of U. S. force; or (3) a true disengagement, an unwillingness to become involved again in the projection of U. S. interests in Asia. He finds the most important clues in the mind and will of the president.

Morton Halperin discusses Japanese reactions to U. S. policies. Many who otherwise would hope for a more relaxed United States posture in Asia are inhibited from arriving at that position through their fear of the course that might be taken by Japan, in the event that the United States relaxed its grip on events in Asia. Halperin talks about the latitude that American policy can assume in Asia and still count on a Japanese reaction that would be constructive and acceptable to the United States. He separates the issues that are of real concern to the Japanese from some of the attitudes that our planners attribute to and project upon the Japanese.

Robert Osgood is benignly critical of the Nixon Doctrine. He accepts its ambiguities as characteristic of a doctrine in its early stages of implementation; the ambiguities are to be normally resolved by actual decisions in response to future contingencies. He would reject an alternative construction grasped by some other contributors: that the ambiguities are actually contradictions, the worst implications of which may be exposed in future attempts to implement the Doctrine. Osgood is candid in identifying a measure of luck as a necessary condition for an ingenious presidential maneuver to bring about a shift in American policy without courting the unsettling international and domestic effects of precipitous action.

John Dower's methodical and factual presentation reveals a multifarious scheme of activity and intention in the Nixon Doctrine that might not be apparent on its surface. His critique proceeds from a rejection of the premise of the legitimacy of the United States national interest in Asia—or, for that matter, any nation's interest anywhere if it stems from social and elite motives that are flawed and potentially dangerous to other, less able, societies. Among other items, Dower is troubled by a certain aspect of the Nixon Doctrine that passes widely for astuteness: its implicit mobilization of latent historical antagonisms and rivalries among East Asian nations in order to continue the fragmentation of the region along the lines of American interests.

Richard Falk's statement implies questions about the level of analysis of a nation's policies. These levels could be described as the instrumental; the diplomatic; and the philosophical, involving morality and national purpose. In his dissection of the national interest in Asia, Falk identifies the various "lessons" that proceed from the American experience in Vietnam that might have led to a temporary and partial consensus on the retrograde movement of American forces. He points out, however, how disparate are the meanings attached to "Never Again," how shallow are some of these meanings, and how their destructive implications might be activated in future contingencies and crises. He points out that the Nixon Doctrine continues, by other instruments, the same philosophy of American domination and interference in the Third World. Tragically, it also narrows the focus of public and bureaucratic attention to the instruments, rather than the philosophy.

Policies and strategies are strongly influenced by the nature of the governmental process and, in some cases, by the technical balance of factors that go into the choice of weapons systems or types of force structure. Procedural or technical details often have effects out of proportion to their apparent significance. The succeeding sections address some of these interior problems, such as military assistance, the derivation of our force structure, and the use of nuclear weapons. These are determinants, as well as elements, of our strategy and our foreign policy.

Leon Sloss, of the State Department, presents the case for the trade-off of military assistance against the use of American ground forces to defend Asian objectives. One of the most important technical aspects of the Nixon Doctrine—in fact the only aspect that begins to emerge with any clarity—is the heavy reliance on military assistance. Official analysis and debate on this issue comprise one of the most distinct cases of the trade-off rationale in the formulation of national security policy. Sloss confirms the apprehension that military assistance is critical to the viability of the Nixon Doctrine. He acknowledges one point as troubling, however: cost-effectiveness as the accepted criterion will lead to a tailoring of forces of the United States and its allies in such a way as to make them complementary, in a true division of labor along the lines of comparative advantage. This might lead to the inextricability of the United States from crisis situations, since it would clearly not be cost-advantageous, for example, to equip South Korea with a self-sufficient air force. Also, since America is a remote—even if involved—power in East Asia (the only one of the prospective quartet of interested great powers that does not impinge geographically), its support must be evidenced by the tangible commitment of American forces—a kind of trip-wire. Implementation of our alliances, it seems, can be made cheaper, but it cannot be made antiseptic.

Pierre Sprey's analysis of the policy consequences of defense management procedures poses the salient paradox: how is it, when they are devoted to rational techniques of organization and decision, that successive administrations come up with such disastrous choices—whether of weapons systems, force structures, or strategies? An answer suggested by Sprey is that, in complex administrative situations, the elaborate structures and procedures are a façade, and that one should look preeminently to the motivational patterns and the incentive structures—that these, indeed, are almost all that matters. He also draws attention to the simplistic analytic basis for force calculation used in the Pentagon, that has never varied from one administration to another: attrition analysis. Sprey documents the internal revolution that has occurred in the Pentagon. The philosophy of "how much is enough," which characterized defense planning under Robert McNamara, has been replaced under Secretary of Defense Laird by a philosophy of prior budgetary constraints. Some feel that the program-budgeting and systems analysis concepts of McNamara have been carelessly abandoned. Others, including many in Congress, join uncritically in a coalition to limit the defense budget on any grounds—even arbitrary ones. But more thought should be given to the net foreign policy implications of budget-constrained forces.

Leonard Rodberg adds the insight—not universally shared —that the Nixon-Laird defense philosophy merely continues and furthers the intervention capabilities of the McNamara era—when they were at their extreme—and is not a throw-back to the Eisenhower era, when U. S. foreign policy was restricted somewhat by the nature of our general purpose forces.

He also believes that the "conventional option" for relatively large wars in Asia and Europe was always a myth—that the "baseline" force was always recognized, even in the McNamara era, as inadequate to forestall recourse to nuclear options.

Stanley Kanarowski talks of tactical nuclear weapons from the vantage point of the army and his experience in developing options in the Defense Department and the National Security Council. Everyone acknowledges the seriousness of the possible drift to nuclear strategies, in view of the logic of the problem. But there are differing assessments of the probability of recourse to nuclear weapons in some future contingency— particularly their first use in response to conventional aggression. The use of tactical nuclear weapons in Asian theaters is a live, debatable issue in the White House, even if the option, upon objective analysis, should not look attractive.

Irrational elements in the national strategy planning process in the White House and the Defense Department emerge in the discussion on "Strategy and the Evolution of 1½ Wars." Discussants both inside and outside the government seem to agree that exhaustive and meticulous strategic analysis was done— and then the decisions were made on entirely different, more expedient, political and economic bases.

Daniel Ellsberg's alarming thesis is that a succession of presidents did not just blunder into the Vietnam quagmire, misled by their bureaucrats and intelligence advisers; rather, another model was operative—thoroughly political in nature and extremely short-term in its horizon (year-to-year, in fact). Ellsberg asks: is there ever a "good" year for a particular president to liquidate the Indochina problem? This thesis, besides contributing insights into the nature of presidential leadership, also holds certain warnings for the future of American intervention under a continuation of presidential decision-making. In addition, Ellsberg hints at a basic fallacy, not only of the Nixon Doctrine, but of a succession of American policies in Asia: the attempt to win Asian victories on the cheap—to resolve the inherent problem of the expense and intractability of the confrontation with China by propagating the myth of the effectiveness of air and naval power, coupled with the shoring up of indigenous armies. Even isolationism, historically, has not meant the abandonment of Asia. On the contrary, it has meant the stubborn refusal to come to terms with the diplomatic problems and the projection of surrealistic means of dealing with the military problems.

Marcus Raskin brings into the calculation some insights into the composition of nations and the nature of the international system. Refuting allegations by the foreign policy establishment of "isolationism," he stresses transnational phenomena and urges a redirection of attention to international restraint and a rebirth of international law. He demands a new set of relationships among groups in the United States as a prerequisite to adjusting our foreign policies. Raskin would read the momentary dissensus that we are experiencing as a challenge to the traditional concept of "national interest."

Considerable distortion is produced in the diction of international relations by the fact that our habit is to talk in the first person plural as international actors—for example, how "we" behave toward the Chinese, what "we" need to do to protect "our" security. We use it almost synonymously with "the government," "the administration," or even at times "the president." Everyone knows that this usage is only a notational convenience, a mere construct. But the usage does subtly connote a consensus or, at least, a single univocal national actor, a national identity. We should be more self-conscious about the first person plural pronoun, even though we continue to use it for convenience. The more important question might be not *"what* are the interests" but *"whose* interests are they." Rather than to nations, more conceivably they belong to movements, classes, or corporations (in the particular and in the general sense). The fact that there are nations need not imply that there are in fact national interests. It may well be that the permanent and objective interests of a body politic are inevitably fragmented and at odds, and that conversely there are larger interest-communities that transcend nations—some with baleful aspects such as we attach to the phenomenon of the trans-national corporation. Yet in this notion of interest-communities that transcend nationality, which we regularly obscure by the convenient notation of our political discussion, there might exist the promise of ultimately dissolving the impasse of statecraft.

Charles Shirkey both asserts and exemplifies the model of deliberate decision-making in a context of constraints. A systems analyst, he deals with the extension of this method to the macro-budgetary level—the world of the president. He treats the pressures and the constraints—the irreconcilables that must be reconciled each year—from the presidential point of view.

Among the principal factors influencing U. S. engagement in Asia, and among the areas in which the consequences of U. S. presence or disengagement will be most felt, is the economic area. The economic question might be defined in three ways: (1) the U.S. stake in Asia; (2) the effects of the U.S. presence, both on allied states and on peripheral communist countries; and (3) the domestic effects of the present United States policy of engagement and the consequences of a major change in that policy—that is, the consequences of disengagement.

Richard Kaufman stresses the currently unfashionable but crucial role of economic motives in the setting of national policies of weapons procurement and foreign intervention. Some have argued that America's economic stakes in Asia are minimal and, therefore, that this country's motives there must be other than economic in nature—perhaps even disinterested. Kaufman attacks this assertion, first by demonstrating through a few well-chosen figures the size of the American economic stake in Asia, and second by emphasizing the power that a concentrated interest group—the arms industry, operating in the encouraging administrative climate established since the end of World War II—can have on policy as well as procurement. Involvement abroad is *not* an economic mistake for the groups that prosper from it. *Their* costs are disproportionately low, and therefore their objective interest in the perpetuation of this investment is disproportionately high.

Seymour Melman talks about the economic consequences of engagement and disengagement. He advocates retrenchment to a basically different security posture—one that excludes preparation for extrahemispheric defense. He argues that tooling up for wars has depleted American industry and infrastructure and squandered the capital of the underdeveloped world. On the other hand, unthinking cutbacks will not restore a balanced, productive economy. The evidence has been that they create vast pools of structural unemployment, not amenable to the classic economic assumption of the mobility of people, jobs, capital, and productive means. Intensive and explicit planning is required for reconversion to an economy of peace.

The discussion of "Approaches to China: Accommodation or Containment?" begins with a review of the evidence of movement in the Nixon administration's China policy, reflecting renewed receptivity to advice from the professional China specialists who had been discredited and intimidated for twenty years. Our military inhibitions and great power pretensions in East Asia, however, might prevent a serious accommodation of China's fundamental interests. Taiwan will be the principal obstacle and challenge.

William Whitson deals with the assessment of the "Chinese threat" and suggests a revision of our concept of containment. Though he holds an orthodox view of the policy requirement for containing China, he argues for a nonprovocative deterrent—one that is adjusted to the reality of China's political and military dispositions and works not to magnify and thus exacerbate the threat, but to reinforce the existing internal constraints that operate on China's leadership. The "threat," in short, derives much from our own identification and judgment of it and the actions we take to counteract it. Whitson is suggesting an important new way of looking at threats, even for the military. It resolves the sterile traditional antithesis of capabilities versus intentions and criticizes the consideration of another country's quantitative capabilities without considering the *direction* of its efforts, military and political (the algebraic sign of the quantity, as it were). China is in many ways *internally* counterbalanced—as are most nations. Therefore, China's political will to use its forces is not infinite.

Franz Schurmann ends the discussion with a trenchant description of the failure of all three variants of U. S. policy in Asia: anticommunist rollback, containment, and even our expansive brand of coexistence. He senses in some recent Chinese initiatives the signaling of a new approach to resolving the problems of Southeast Asia. China, according to Schurmann, has put forth a signal involving Prince Sihanouk of Cambodia: the Chinese have used Sihanouk as a symbol of their willingness to settle for coalition governments in Southeast Asia. By being sensitive, and responding sensibly, to such approaches, Schurmann believes the United States could attain, not a trouble-free, but a viable, settlement of the Indochina conflict, and an end to the "permanent confrontation with China."

Two functional poles are represented by the contributors: the radical policy critic and the government servant—"the yogi and the commissar." And there are two fundamental ways in which these polar types of participants differ: first, in their conception of the *history* of policy; second, in their conception of the *process* of policy.

Those who have served, particularly recently, in the executive bureaucracy tend to view the history of policy as cyclical —an alternation of intervention and isolation, engagement and disengagement. They accept the periodicity of "great debates"—and they are ready to adjust to them, to make those pragmatic, minimal accommodations that allow administrative continuity and departmental integrity; that allow them to hold their positions and handle the details of their daily work. This tolerant cyclical conception of policy history is in reality a neutralization of it—rendering it devoid of significance; treating it as transient fashion or style.

On the other hand, the historical view of the radical policy critics, whether doctrinaire or independent, is secular: that there is a meaningful procession of stages, with an underlying and necessary continuity of purpose that reflects the character of a nation, a society, or a group. Historical motives, implicit in the character of certain kinds of society or leadership, determine their actions.

There are correlative differences in attitudes toward the decision-making process, which represents individual and institutional actions of choice within the historical context. The bureaucrats see decisions as willed, as the effects of deliberation and rational choice, within certain constraints. They see themselves as operating decisively among options, responding to the explicit features of situations. They would not readily admit that they themselves are part of the process and as determined as their environments or their resources. "Policy science," in the narrower and more utilitarian sense of an adjunct to rational decision-making, is a welcome discipline to the bureaucratic professionals. To them, it often takes the form of systems analysis, which is an idealization of deliberate choice.

The contrary view of the radical critics and scholars, who are outside of and abstracted from the process, is rather one of a "science of policy," as opposed to a "policy science." They see the decision-makers as themselves enmeshed in the gears of the policy process: they are not simply constrained; they are determined, just as their environment and materials are determined. Their decisions are intelligible only when seen as events, rather than as judgments of events.

Both sets of contrary theoretical tendencies—the cyclical

or the secular view of history, and the deliberate or the determined view of decision—need some further examination of the structures, or the mechanisms, through which these larger necessities are transmitted into particular actions. There must be some causal, or operational, linkage that can be identified. Part of the answer is in identifying motivational patterns, and their obverse: incentives. Another part of the answer is the structure through which a motivational scheme expresses itself and through which institutions maintain and perpetuate their motivational patterns and codify and enforce their preferences. That part of the answer lies in a detailed tracing of the nature of action systems—bureaucracies and decision-making networks. The excursion, in this book, into "Decision-making for Asia: Options or Compulsions?" may throw some light on these elements of the policy process.

There is another kind of problem—a challenge for policy analysis—that inheres in the multiple significances of policy statements or doctrines. The popular shorthand expression of this problem is that the statements are "ambiguous." But this would imply that the "ambiguities" can be adjusted by the clearer use of words. I would suggest, on the contrary, that (1) in one sense, the ambiguities and unclarities are an irreplaceable *part* of the meaning; and (2) in another sense, even the clearest statements can be *objectively* without meaning, in that they may be at odds with circumstances that control future situations.

A policy statement might have meaning on several levels:

1. *The rhetorical:* what the words seem to say.

2. *The declaratory:* what its authors intend to have believed—either the public-relations aspect (the mobilization of support) or the diplomatic aspect (the conveyance of bargaining signals).

3. *The intentional:* what its authors intend for themselves —what we have a right to infer about this; what they would do as a consequence of making the statement; what they prefer.

4. *The instrumental:* how the implementing agencies (and adversaries) will interpret the policy or statement; the license or stimulus it will provide—these are closer to the operational questions.

5. *The structural:* what it *can* mean, or what it *must* mean; the situational logic (including the constraints as well as the options, the resources as well as the intentions)—this meaning becomes the model of the whole policy process.

In terms of the last, most comprehensive, interpretation of the meaning of a policy or a doctrine, the scope and intent of this book becomes evident: it is an attempt to elicit the meaning of policy—particularly U. S. policy toward China—by examining the relationships among the elements of the policy process. This activity borders on the function of prophecy. For prophets do not predict, in the sense of guessing the future; rather, they demonstrate relationships—tangible, intellectual, moral. They construct—or reconstruct—a universe, rearranging the elements in it, laying out the "if-then" relationships that actually exist. And, although "if-then" is a future calculation, they apply it also to the present, and even to the past. The prophets say, in effect, to the kings and the statesmen: you did this, and that happened; how else did you expect it to turn out, since these (A,B,C,D) were the elements in the situation? They interpret—or sum up—the actual moves and pronounce what the "tangible" commitment actually is; which direction has implicitly been chosen; what alternatives can no longer be entertained; what options have in fact been foregone.

The problems for U. S. strategy in Asia have not been solved —they have merely been postponed—by the Nixon administration. There have been initiatives, but these have been inconclusive. Furthermore, the structure of the situation has not changed. Even a more fundamental shift in direction by this government will have to be a choice within the possibilities that the situation realistically provides.

The contributions in this book, then, will continue to have significance, because they deal with the basic relationships between institutions and policy outputs, attitudes and behavior. They suggest the shape of national action. If they embody accurate description, meaningful insight, and sound analysis, they will lead to useful predictions. And if they discover and enlighten profound and fundamental relationships, they will be a kind of prophecy.

II

THE NIXON DOCTRINE:

DISENGAGEMENT OR CONFRONTATION?

The Nixon Doctrine, Defense Policy, and China

EARL C. RAVENAL: The Nixon Doctrine is not the formula for peace with China or stability in Asia. Long after its enunciation at Guam, it remains obscure and contradictory in its intent and application. It is not simply that the wider pattern of war in Indochina challenges the Doctrine's promise of a lower posture in Asia. More than that, close analysis and the unfolding of events expose some basic flaws in the logic of the Nixon administration's evolving security policy for the new decade. The Nixon Doctrine properly includes more than the declaratory policy orientation. It comprises also the revised worldwide security strategy of "1½ wars" and the new defense decision-making processes such as "fiscal guidance budgeting." These elements have received little comment, especially in their integral relation to our commitments in Asia. But the effects of the Nixon administration's moves in these areas will shape and constrain the choices of the United States for a long time to come.

President Nixon's first foreign policy declaration of February 1970 promised that "our interests, our foreign policy objectives, our strategies and our defense budgets are being brought into balance—with each other and with our overall national priorities." [1] After a decade of burgeoning military

1. Richard Nixon, *U. S. Foreign Policy for the 1970's, A New Strategy for Peace,* February 18, 1970.

spending and entanglement in foreign conflict, the nation has welcomed the vision of lower defense budgets balanced by a reduction in American involvement overseas, particularly in Asia. Actually, however, the Nixon Administration's new policies and decision processes do not bring about the proposed balance; in fact, they create a more serious imbalance. Essentially we are to support the same level of potential involvement with smaller conventional forces. The specter of intervention will remain, but the risk of defeat or stalemate will be greater; or the nuclear threshold will be lower. The fundamental issues of interests, commitments and alliances are not resolved.

The Strategy Problem

The objectives of close-in military containment and the forward defense of our Asian allies present us with a series of bleak choices:

With regard to deterrence: (1) perpetuation of a high level of active conventional forces, conspicuously deployed or deployable; (2) fundamental and obvious reliance on nuclear weapons; or (3) acknowledgment of the higher probability of an enemy initiative.

With regard to initial defense: (1) maintenance or rapid deployment of large armies in Asia; (2) early recourse to tactical nuclear weapons; or (3) acceptance of the greater risk of losing allied territory.

With regard to terminating a war: (1) large commitments of troops and heavy casualties; (2) use of nuclear weapons, either tactical or strategic; or (3) resignation to an indefinite and wasting stalemate, tantamount to defeat.

The only solution that transcends the triangle of unsatisfactory choices is to reevaluate our interests in Asia; restate those objectives that implicate us in the possibility of war on the Asian mainland and diminish our control over our actions; resist the grand and vapid formulas of our role in Asia—such

as the existential platitude that "we are a Pacific power"—
that perpetuate the illusion of paramountcy; retreat from the
policy of military containment of China; and revise the alliances that have come to represent our commitment to containment.

But this course President Nixon has consistently rejected:
". . . we will maintain our interests in Asia and the commitments that flow from them. . . . The United States will keep
all its treaty commitments." Thus the root problem of the
Nixon Doctrine is its abiding commitment to the containment
of China. In the furtherance of this policy our government
hopes to maintain all our present Asian alliances and de facto
commitments, profiting from their deterrent value but avoiding their implications. Yet it also intends to scale down our
conventional military capability. The result is that the Nixon
Doctrine neither reduces our potential involvement in Asian
conflicts nor resolves the resulting dilemma by providing con-
vincingly for a defense that will obviate reliance on nuclear
weapons.

Let us examine the prospect of the Nixon Doctrine as a re-
lief from involvement in Asian contingencies. The trauma that
has resulted from our inability to win decisively in Vietnam
has caused our policy-makers to suggest a limitation of future
involvement on the basis of a distinction between external or
overt aggression on the one hand, and insurgency, political
subversion, and civil war on the other. President Nixon attempts in this way to avoid the strategy dilemma by altering
the criteria for intervention and thus understating the probability of involvement:

> . . . we cannot expect U. S. military forces to cope with the
> entire spectrum of threats facing allies or potential allies
> throughout the world. This is particularly true of subversion
> and guerrilla warfare, or "wars of national liberation." Expe-
> rience has shown that the best means of dealing with insur-
> gencies is to preempt them through economic development
> and social reform and to control them with police, paramili-
> tary and military action by the threatened government.

But this is nothing more than a postulation that the unwished contingency will not arise. The hard question remains: what if these "best means" are not successful? Under *those* conditions what kind of solutions does the Nixon Doctrine envisage? Might the United States be impelled to intervene with combat forces? Nixon states:

> . . . a direct combat role for U. S. general purpose forces arises primarily when insurgency has shaded into external aggression or when there is an overt conventional attack. In such cases, we shall weigh our interests and our commitments, and we shall consider the efforts of our allies, in determining our response.

But this formula for discrimination and discretion seems both unclear and unrealistic. At what point does an insurgency become "external aggression"? A definition sometimes proposed is the introduction of enemy main-force units, rather than mere individual fillers. But, even apart from the difficult question of verification, this event might be well beyond the point where our intervention became critical to the situation. The paradox is that in critical cases we might not wish to define the situation to preclude intervention; in less than critical cases we would not need to invoke nice distinctions to justify it. In any case, relying on formulas and distinctions misses the point: it is simply not credible that we would sacrifice our still-held objectives to the vagaries of circumstance.

Indeed, as long as our policy remains—in any guise or formulation—the containment of China and the repression of Asian communism, we are inclined to view even largely indigenous revolutions as objective instances of the purposes of Peking or Hanoi or Pyongyang. Consequently, if an insurgency in an allied or even a neutral country began to succeed, we would probably first increase logistical aid, then extend the role of advisers and provide air support. Since such moves might bring a countervailing response from the Asian communist sponsors of the insurgency, we might have to choose between sending ground forces and allowing an ally to lose by our default. In certain extremities we might be forced to the final choice among unlimited conventional escalation, defeat of our own forces, or "technological escalation" to the use of nuclear weapons.

Thus, with our formal or implied commitments and Nixon's open-ended prescription, the United States might yet be drawn into a land war on the Asian mainland or have to confront equally dire alternatives. In this respect the Nixon Doctrine does not improve on the policy that led to Vietnam. And, of course, our exposure to involvement in the case of more overt aggression, such as a Chinese-supported invasion in Korea or Southeast Asia, remains undiminished.

The only proposition that has become clear about the Nixon Doctrine is that its most advertised hope of resolving the strategy problem—both reducing the forces we maintain for Asian defense and avoiding involvement in conflict—is Asianization, i.e. the substitution of indigenous forces, equipped through enlarged U. S. military assistance, for American troops. The case for expanded military assistance has been stated with unprecedented urgency by Secretary Laird in preparation for vastly increased Military Assistance Program (MAP) budget requests for 1972 and succeeding fiscal years. Secretary Laird has characterized MAP as "the essential ingredient of our policy if we are to honor our obligations, support our allies, and yet reduce the likelihood of having to commit American ground combat units." [2]

But Laird recognizes the declining level of popular and congressional support for military assistance. His solution, considered perennially within the Defense and State Departments but proposed for the first time in a secretarial posture statement to the Congress, is that "military assistance should be integrated into the defense budget so that we can plan more rationally and present to the Congress more fully an in-

2. Melvin R. Laird, *Fiscal Year 1971 Defense Program and Budget* (Washington, D. C.: U. S. Government Printing Office, March 2, 1970).

tegrated program." Military aid for certain "forward defense countries," including South Vietnam, Thailand, and Laos, and consisting of about 80 percent of the total category "Support for Other Nations," [3] is already meshed into the defense budget. This legislative ploy has not yet been applied to Korea or Taiwan, though the reduction of our troops in Korea and the insurance of Taiwan against communist pressure depend, in the judgment of the Nixon administration, on the freedom to substitute U. S. material for manpower.

To merge military assistance entirely into the regular functional appropriation categories of the defense budget would be to institutionalize the dual rationale for military assistance that has become traditional in debate within the Department of Defense. The first element in this rationale is the argument from "trade-off"—a calculus that compares the costs of equal units of effectiveness of U. S. and foreign troops. This is essentially an assertion of "absolute advantage" and is the basic and obvious sense of Secretary Laird's statement: "A MAP dollar is of far greater value than a dollar spent directly on U. S. forces."

The second element is the argument from "comparative advantage," borrowed from the economic theory of international trade: "Each nation must do its share and contribute what it can appropriately provide—manpower from many of our allies; technology, material, and specialized skills from the United States." The proponents of military comparative advantage assert, by analogy, that the cooperating and specializing defense community can "consume" security at a higher level. It may be, however, that they can only consume more of the tangible intermediate trappings of security, that is, the forces and arms. The essence of security, especially for the United States as the senior partner, might depend more on certain qualitative factors. In fact, there are several difficulties

3. $2.443 billion out of $3.127 billion in the president's budget for fiscal year 1971.

in these ostensibly neutral and technical arguments for military assistance.

First, both trade-off and comparative advantage assume and confirm the inevitability and relevance of the shared mission—that is, the forward defense of the ally's territory. But only if we cannot avoid this mission is it proper to confine the debate to the optimal distribution of roles and costs.

Second, the argument from comparative advantage, like the economic theory at its origin, stresses specialization. But the concomitant of specialization is interdependence. Thus a policy of selective reliance on allies, in order to be effective, implies automatic involvement from the earliest moments of a conflict.[4]

Third, early experience indicates that U. S. ground forces cannot simply be traded off with precisely calculated increments of military assistance. They must be politically ransomed by disproportionate grants, more conspicuous deployments and more fervent and explicit confirmations of our commitment.[5]

Fourth, from the diplomatic standpoint the substitution of massive infusions of modern arms for U. S. troops is anything but neutral. To the North Koreans and their sponsors, for example, the one and one-half billion dollars of support and new equipment we now intend to give South Korea might look very provocative and destabilizing. A new phase of the

4. After the decision to reduce the ceiling on U. S. troops in Korea from 63,000 to 43,000, our government moved to base permanently there a wing of F-4 fighter-bombers. An American official explained: "Our aim is to re-assure the Koreans during this difficult period. Despite budgetary cuts, it shows we intend to maintain our relative air strength here. They know that the minute an air attack starts, we're involved." (*The New York Times,* August 17, 1970.)

5. The Nixon administration proposes special budget requests of $1 billion over a five-year period for Korean force modernization, in addition to about $700 million likely to be provided in the regular military assistance budget. Even then, the Republic of Korea is demanding $2–3 billion, plus public assurances of no further troop withdrawals until after five years and the actual completion of the promised modernization program.

peninsular arms race could be the result, with a net loss to regional and U. S. security.

Finally, the legislative tactic of integrating the Military Assistance Program into the defense budget would remove military assistance as an object of the broader concerns of foreign policy and assign it to the jurisdiction of more narrowly defense-oriented congressional committees. The debate would be less political and more technical. The focus would shift from the question of involvement to the question of relative costs. Thus Asianization, which is the keystone of the Nixon Doctrine, would substitute some Asian forces and resources, but along the same perimeter of interest. It affords a pretext for reducing expense, but it does not enhance our security or relieve us from involvement.

The basic question is whether the Nixon Doctrine is an honest policy that will fully fund the worldwide and Asian commitments it proposes to maintain, or whether it conceals a drift toward nuclear defense or an acceptance of greater risk of local defeat. The most obvious change in our military posture is that the new formula provides conventional forces to counter a major communist thrust in Asia or Europe, but not simultaneously. As President Nixon has explained:

> The stated basis of our conventional posture in the 1960's was the so-called "2½ war" principle. According to it, U. S. forces would be maintained for a three-month conventional forward defense of NATO, a defense of Korea or Southeast Asia against a full-scale Chinese attack, and a minor contingency—all simultaneously. These force levels were never reached.
>
> In the effort to harmonize doctrine and capability, we chose what is best described as the "1½ war" strategy. Under it we will maintain in peacetime general purpose forces adequate for simultaneously meeting a major Communist attack in either Europe or Asia, assisting allies against

non-Chinese threats in Asia, and contending with a contingency elsewhere.

What will be the ultimate force levels associated with the new 1½ war strategy, and how can we assess their implications for Asian defense? Peacetime forces are obviously entailed by the extent of our commitments, but in no precisely determined way. A most important intermediate term—which could account for wide differences in strategy and forces—is the probable simultaneity of contingencies.[6] The Nixon strategy of 1½ wars is explicitly founded on the improbability of two simultaneous major contingencies. Thus demands on the planned general purpose forces are to' be considered alternative rather than additive.

Can we then expect an eventual force reduction equivalent to the requirement for defending against the lesser of the major contingencies? To support the previous strategy of 2½ wars, the Baseline (or peacetime) Force Structure was thought to provide 7 active divisions for Southeast Asia, 2 for Korea, 8 for NATO, and 2⅓ for a minor contingency and a strategic reserve—a total of 19⅓. Since the present 1½ war doctrine includes only one major contingency, in NATO *or* Asia, one might derive an active ground force as low as 10⅓ divisions.

Such a literal expectation, however, is confused by President Nixon's desire to insure "against greater than expected threats by maintaining more than the forces required to meet conventional threats in one theater—such as NATO Europe"; the fact that certain types of divisions are inherently specialized for certain geographical contingencies, so that all eight of our armored and mechanized divisions will probably remain oriented to NATO and inapplicable to Asian defense;· and finally, the judgments of both President Nixon and Secretary

6. Other sources of uncertainty and wide variation are: the readiness of our reserve divisions, the amount of available airlift and sealift, and the effectiveness of allied forces.

Laird that the force levels necessary to implement the previous 2½ war policy "were never reached."

But it seems clear that the ultimate Baseline Force Structure under the Nixon Doctrine will contain even fewer divisions for the Asian requirement than the minimal proposals
for a conventional defense.[7] The reduced conventional force is
most significant as a reflection of the altered concept of Asian
defense embodied in the Nixon Doctrine. The constituent
propositions of this concept are: (1) the most likely threats to
our Asian allies do not involve Chinese invasion, and (2) with
greatly expanded military assistance our allies can largely provide the ground forces to counter such threats.

There is a third proposition, strongly implied by the logic
of the problem and markedly signaled in the Nixon foreign
policy statement: in a future Asian conflict, particularly if it
does involve China, United States intervention is likely to
carry with it the use of tactical nuclear weapons.

> the nuclear capability of our strategic and theater nuclear
> forces serves as a deterrent to full-scale Soviet attack on
> NATO Europe or Chinese attack on our Asian allies;
>
> the prospects for a coordinated two-front attack on our allies
> by Russia and China are low both because of the risks of nu-
> clear war and the improbability of Sino-Soviet cooperation.
> In any event, we do not believe that such a coordinated at-
> tack should be met primarily by U. S. conventional forces.

Though the "coordinated" attack described by President
Nixon is improbable, it should be noted that "theater nuclear
forces" are prescribed as deterrents against the *single* contingency of a "Chinese attack on our Asian allies." Also, there
are more plausible scenarios that would, in terms of their po-

---

7. About five to seven divisions have been considered the minimum to
blunt and delay an attack along the main access routes in Southeast Asia,
then fall back to a defensible perimeter. Against a communist invasion of
Korea it was thought that the South Korean army alone could hold initially north of Seoul until reinforced by Korean reserves or U. S. units to
be mobilized or diverted from other requirements.

tential to immobilize U. S. forces, be the functional equivalent of a major attack: a Soviet military build-up and political pressure in central or southern Europe; or China's rendering massive logistical support to one of her Asian allies to the point where that ally could release overwhelming forces against a neighboring country; or the imminent entry of China into a war where we or one of our allies might have provided the provocation. It is conceivable that two such lesser contingencies could arise, in Europe and Asia, and that one of them could develop to the point of a conflict. In that event we would be reluctant to consider our conventional forces for either theater available for the other. Motivated by illusions of decisive action and immunity from retaliation, we might be tempted to dispose of the Asian conflict by technological escalation.

Therefore, if we remain committed to the defense of interests in both theaters, but maintain conventional forces for only one large contingency, our strategy is biased toward the earlier use of nuclear weapons. Of course, there is no necessary continuum of escalation from conventional war to tactical nuclear war. But the 1½ war strategy provides a president with fewer alternatives and renders the resort to nuclear weapons a more compelling choice, as well as making nuclear threat a more obvious residual feature of our diplomacy.

And so the "balance" promised in the new security policy is achieved—but not by adjusting our commitments, restricting our objectives, or modifying our conception of the interests of the United States. Rather, budgetary stringencies inspire a reduction in force levels; a "1½ war strategy" is tailored to fit the intractable realities; and a series of rationalizations is constructed to validate the new strategy—rationalizations that simply stipulate a reduced threat, count heavily on subsidized and coerced allied efforts at self-defense, and suggest an early nuclear reaction if our calculations prove insufficiently conservative.

Thus the Nixon Doctrine reveals a contradiction between

objectives and strategy. Are we seeing the beginning of a return to the defense posture of the 1950s, with unabated commitments to a collection of frontline client-states, but with limited options and a renewed flirtation with the fantasy of tactical nuclear warfare?

The Defense Planning Process

The new security policy not only shifts substantively down to a 1½ war strategy but also changes the model for determining defense requirements. Instead of the classic progression from the definition of foreign policy interests to the formulation of objectives, to the prescription of strategies, to the calculation of forces and their costs, we now see a constrained calculus that proceeds in reverse from limited budgets to trimmed forces to arbitrary strategies. The implications are not transmitted through the system to include a revision of objectives and interests. At best the system is balanced back from resources through strategies; the imbalance is shifted to a point between strategies and objectives.

But even the strategies and the forces may be out of balance. For the budget-constrained strategy revision is complemented by a fundamental change in the defense planning process. The previous system was requirements-oriented: there was, in theory, no prior budgetary restriction. Rather, planning began with our stated worldwide defense objectives and resulted in forces and a budget which were recommended to the president and the Congress as systematically entailed by those objectives. Of course, the ideal system foundered on the institutional realities of weapons-system and force creation. Indeed, the philosophy of unconstrained implementation of security objectives—"buy what you need"—encouraged inflated requirements within the framework of 2½ wars. And the attempts of the secretary to limit forces only led the military to attempts to goldplate those prescribed forces, while keeping a ledger on the "shortfall" between the imposed strategy and the imposed force structure. But at least the direction and scope of the planning process compelled attention to the relevance and adequacy of the forces, and allowed the possibility of reasoning back from the rejection of excessive requirements to the questioning of overambitious strategies, extensive commitments, and artificial interests.

By contrast, the new defense planning process begins simultaneously with "strategic guidance" and "fiscal guidance," established by the president and the National Security Council. The new procedure has attained certain efficiencies in managing the Pentagon budget cycle. But from the policy standpoint it is completely existential: within the fiscal ceilings we will get the forces and weapons systems that the organization tends to produce—not the ones we might need. Of the two kinds of guidance, the fiscal is quantitative and unarguable; the strategic is verbal and elastic. If there is a coincidence of those forces and systems tailored to the fiscal guidance and those derived from the strategic guidance, it will be either accidental or contrived.

More likely, the Services will interpret the new guidance as a set of parameters within which they can promote self-serving programs. Under conditions of budgetary stringency they will skimp on manpower, supplies, war reserve stocks, maintenance, and transport, while preserving headquarters, cadres of units, research and development of large new systems, and sophisticated technological overhead. In effect they will tend, as in the 1950s, to sacrifice those items that maintain balance, readiness, and sustainability of effort, and to insist on those items that insure morale, careers, and the competitive position of each Service.

Thus the Nixon administration's defense planning procedure allows a second contradiction: between strategy and forces. This country may well end the 1970s with the worst of both worlds: on the one hand, a full panoply of commitments and a strategy that continues to serve an ambitious policy of containment; on the other, a worldwide sprinkling of token deployments and a force structure that is still expensive, but unbalanced, unready, and irrelevant to our security.

Alliances and Containment

The disabilities of the Nixon Doctrine follow from its insistence on the containment of China in face of budgetary pressures that arise not out of absolute scarcity of resources, but out of the nation's unwillingness to make large sacrifices for objectives that cannot be credibly invoked by its leadership. If the administration is to be consistent in revising our defense posture and limiting defense budgets, it must consider a commensurate curtailment of our foreign policy objectives in Asia. Adjusting the intermediate term—the strategies—will not effect the reconciliation and permit an honest implementation of the force and budget cuts.

But the Nixon Doctrine does not resolve the Asian defense problem in this fundamental way: rather, it appears as another formula for permanent confrontation with China. What are the issues that elude the perennial expressions of interest, by several administrations, in accommodating China? During the Johnson administration the policy of containment ceded to a variant characterized as "containment without isolation." The shift, however, was accompanied by no tangible initiatives and induced no reciprocity from China. President Nixon entered office with a mandate—which he had created largely himself through his campaign emphasis—to bring about a reconciliation with China. His administration has relaxed certain restrictions on trade and travel and revived the Warsaw ambassadorial talks. But such moves, though impressive as indications of enlightenment, do not touch on the essential concerns of China. However we ultimately conceive our interests, we might as well be realistic about the eventual price of a real accommodation with China.

This price would include three kinds of consideration: (1) diplomatic recognition and admission without qualification to the United Nations and the permanent Security Council seat; (2) most important—affirmation of a one-China policy, allowing the eventual accession of Taiwan to the mainland; (3) removal of the U. S. military presence on Taiwan and the mainland of Asia, without substituting a naval cordon, a ring of nearby island bases, a host of Asian mercenary armies, or a nuclear tripwire. The components of such a withdrawal would be: liquidation of the Vietnam war and removal of all U. S. forces there; retraction of all U. S. troops from other mainland Asian countries and Taiwan and closure of all bases; termination of military assistance to the Republic of China and mainland states and cessation of efforts to create proxy forces to continue our mission; and dissolution of our security alliances with the "forward-defense" countries of Thailand, Taiwan, and Korea.

Such a program would amount to a major diplomatic revolution. It might take a decade or a quarter of a century to implement, even with the most sophisticated public and political support within the United States. It would alienate client regimes, unsettle for long intervals our relations with the Soviets, and tax the understanding of major allies such as Japan and Australia. It would signify the renunciation of our efforts to control events in Asia; henceforth we would control only our responses to events.

But it is fair to ask whether we will not arrive at this disposition of affairs in Asia at some point, whether we will it or not. Should this occur after a quarter of a century of tension and devastation, or political maneuver and diplomatic search? It is also fair to speculate that a more neutral, or even positive, relationship with China might give us a new scope of advantages. We might benefit eventually from a commercial relationship with China, rather than conceding the economic penetration of the mainland by Japan and Western Europe while we remain frozen in our historic impasse. We might also, simply through the dissolution of predictable enmity with China, make it more difficult for the Soviets to challenge us in other areas of the world. And we might find it useful to have a counterpoise to Japan, which is still our principal Pacific competitor, economic and potentially military, and a possible future partner of the USSR in such common interests as counterbalancing China and developing eastern Siberia.

The tangible expressions of containment are our security alliances and the other strong, though less formal, military commitments around the periphery of China. These commitments, it can be argued, *create* the threat to us by transforming otherwise neutral events into situations of relevance to our interests; perpetuate the confrontation with China that gives substance to the threat, by frustrating the essential motives of China; lock us into a posture of forward defense on the mainland of Asia; and dictate the requirement for large general-purpose forces or equivalent means of deterrence and defense.

Our alliances in Asia do not form a coherent and comprehensive system such as NATO. Rather thay are a collection of bilateral agreements, plus the multilateral SEATO pact, contracted separately from 1951 through 1962. Even the purposes served by these alliances, as seen at the time of their negotiation, were diverse. Containment of China might have been a concurrent motive, but it did not uniformly inspire the creation of the pacts. Quite apart from containing our enemies, several of the treaties exhibit motives of containing our allies as well.

The ANZUS (Australia-New Zealand-United States) and Philippine treaties of 1951, though signed against the backdrop of the Korean War, related more to the fear of Japan which these allies derived from World War II. The 1953 agreement with the Republic of Korea was, among other things, a price for Syngman Rhee's restraint from attempting to reunify the peninsula by force. Similarly the treaty with the Republic of China in 1954 was in part a quid pro quo for Chiang's acceptance of "releashing" during the Straits crisis of that year. The SEATO alliance of 1954, which extended protection to South Vietnam, Laos, and Cambodia, arose less from the vision of true collective defense than the desire of the United States to have a legal basis for discretionary intervention under the nominal coloration of "united action." The bilateral U. S.-Thai adjunct to SEATO, negotiated by Rusk and Thanat in 1962, reassured the Thais, during the events that led to the Laos neutralization accords, that the U. S. would respond to a threat to Thai security, regardless of the reaction of other SEATO signatories; this agreement, too, was a price to secure the acquiescence of an ally in an arrangement that suited the interest of the United States. The 1960 Security Treaty with Japan partially adjusted the original unequal treaty of 1951, reaffirmed U. S. administration of Okinawa and perpetuated our use of bases in the Japanese home islands, subject to prior consultation for nuclear or direct combat deployments. (The Nixon-Sato communiqué of October 1969 pledged reversion of Okinawa to Japan by 1972, a status that implies removal of nuclear weapons and submission to the "homeland formula" for consultation on the use of bases.)

Though deterrence of China became the primary function of our alliances, their military content has changed profoundly from the time they were contracted. The Dulles policy, in the pacts of 1953–1954, did not emphasize the actual defense of allied territory or contemplate the dispatch of U. S. ground forces to any point where the communist powers chose to apply military force. Rather, it aimed at nuclear deterrence of overt aggression—punishment rather than geographical denial. In this concept the alliances served to establish a territorial definition. The implied countermeasure was the discretionary application of American nuclear force against communist airfields, supply centers, ports, and perhaps industries and cities. The concept was not clearly resolved: it was semistrategic and semitactical, partially punitive and partially for direct military effect. Also, cases short of obvious aggression, such as subversion and support for internal revolutionary struggles, were acknowledged to be imprecise and difficult. In

Indochina in 1954 the Eisenhower administration could not identify an appropriate enemy or target to fit the massive nuclear response and narrowly declined to intervene. Of course, it also sensed the lack of formal alliance protection over Southeast Asia as an impediment to intervention and moved to create SEATO within two months of the partition of Vietnam.

The refinement of tactical battlefield nuclear weapons in the middle and later 1950s made conceivable the notion of actual nuclear defense confined to the theater of conflict. The Kennedy-McNamara policy of flexible response, including counterinsurgency techniques and large balanced conventional forces, finally provided the practical means of containing a full spectrum of Chinese or Chinese-supported initiatives. Thus the policy of close-in containment of China acquired its maximum content of actual forward defense of allied territory.

Under the Nixon Doctrine, this defensive content will recede from its high water mark. There is a set of propositions that qualifies military deterrence: the more explicit and obvious our commitment, the more effective in preventing war, but the less effective in preventing our involvement in war; conversely, the more attenuated our commitment, the less certain our involvement, but the more probable a hostile initiative.

An administration with a more relaxed view of Asia might take the risk of the second proposition and look more neutrally on a communist probe. But the Nixon administration appears likely to maintain its deterrent stance and take its chances on involvement in conflict. This would mean that it will not overtly diminish any commitment; indeed it is likely to reaffirm and reinforce any commitment that is beset by doubt. But to maintain the deterrent effect of our commitments in the face of reductions in budgets, forces, and deployments, it must replace deleted capabilities with some equivalent, such as increased rapid deployment ability or nuclear threat. The Nixon administration could not count entirely on the mobility of our forces, which can be evidenced only by massive exercises and adequate lift resources, which are far from certain to be appropriated. Residually, it is forced to rely on nuclear deterrence, which need only be hinted.

So our mode of deterrence and our provisions for defense will now progressively diverge from the preferences of our treaty partners. Our proposed substitution of technology and threat for our manpower and presence might be equivalent from our point of view, but not from that of our allies. None of our Asian defense arrangements is specific about the tangible support that might be evoked by an act of aggression. No joint defense force with agreed war plans and command structures exists. Our military concept could become, rather than the forward defense of all territory, a mobile defense, an enclave strategy, or even a nuclear tripwire. In another dimension, our commitment might be satisfied by various types of support, such as logistical, tactical air, or nuclear fire. U. S. contingency plans are essentially unilateral and subject to uncommunicated change. And implementation of all treaties refers to our constitutional procedures, which are themselves in a phase of more stringent interpretation.

Because of this scope for maneuver or evasion, our Asian allies will be correspondingly more sensitive to interpretive commentary by U. S. officials and to shifts in our military posture. Already they sense that the substantive content of our alliances is affected by President Nixon's choice of worldwide strategy. The selected strategy is described as defending both Europe and Asia—though alternatively. But it is clear that Europe holds priority and claims virtually as many resources as previously; the major war case associated with the reduction in active forces is Asia. Although no alliances are formally disturbed, our Asian allies, as they count our divisions and analyze our posture statements and policy declarations, have cause for concern that behind the façade of ritualistic reiteration we might have altered our capability and specific intent to fulfill our treaty commitments.

Thus we can devalue the diplomatic and deterrent effect of our alliances without even gaining immunity from involvement, simply by shifting strategies, debating criteria for intervention and making arbitrary adjustments in force levels. In view of the liabilities of this course—which is the course of the Nixon administration—we might as well face the problem more directly and begin to consider the broader alternatives to containment of China, with their full implications for our alliances in Asia.

Conclusion

As long as we assert interests in Asia that (1) entail defending territory, (2) could plausibly be threatened by hostile actions, and (3) are evidenced by alliances that dispose us to a military response, we are exposed to the contingency of involvement. If we maintain this exposure through insistence on our present Asian commitments, while adopting budget-constrained strategies, we risk a future defeat or stalemate, or we allow ourselves to be moved toward reliance on nuclear weapons.

To avoid these alternatives, two courses are available. One is heavy dependence on allied forces to fulfill defense requirements. This is the hope of Asianization, offered prominently by the Nixon Doctrine. But this policy binds us closely to the fate of our Asian clients and diminishes our control over our involvement; and there is still the liability that U. S. forces might be required to rescue the efforts of our allies.

The other course is a process of military readjustment and political accommodation that would make it far less likely that we would become involved every time there is some slippage in the extensive diplomatic "fault" that runs along the rim of Asia. This course is arduous and complex, and as little under our unilateral and absolute control as a course of military deterrence. But the consequences of not budging from our present set of ambitions and illusions—or of trifling with the unalterable purposes of China by limiting ourselves to insubstantial diplomatic initiatives—are far bleaker.

The situation calls not for a symbolic shift in strategy—such as the 1½ war doctrine—which is founded on the hope that the contingencies that would test it, to which we are still liable, might not occur. The situation is not amenable to purely instrumental solutions, such as the calculated equippage of allied armies or the reliance on technological escalation. The situation requires a fundamental questioning and revision of the containment of China.

The confusion that surrounds the Nixon Doctrine is appropriate to its conflicting message and incomplete intent. While pledging to honor all of our existing commitments, President Nixon has placed them all in considerable doubt. While offering promise of avoiding involvement in future Asian conflicts, he has simply biased the nature of our participation. Thus, in the attempt to perpetuate our control of the destiny of Asia, the Nixon Doctrine may forfeit control of our own destiny in Asia.

The Rhetoric and
the Reality of Disengagement

LESLIE H. GELB: I would like to make three points. First, as for what you do practically to disengage the United States from Asia, I would do roughly what the Nixon administration is doing. Second, I am not sure the Nixon administration means the same things by what it is doing that *I* would hope it means. And third, even if I had the confidence that they did mean the same things that I would want them to mean, I think academicians ought to assume a critical set, to insure that pressure is maintained on the administration to make things come out the way we would like, or at least to make them justify what they are doing.

On the first point, I think the Nixon administration is doing about the right thing as far as the whole sweep of Asia policy is concerned. When you put all the pieces together they make a fairly formidable tapestry of change. Negotiations have been completed on the principle of reversion of Okinawa. We are closing bases in Japan. We are taking troops out of Thailand. We are taking the equivalent of 20,000 men out of Korea. Men are being withdrawn from Vietnam—not as quickly as I would like, not with a definite time schedule, but they are being taken out. (I think the Vietnamization policy is a wrong one, but men are coming out.) Attempts are being made to reformulate our military and economic assistance to Asian countries. Measures have been taken to relax restrictions against China.

The Nixon Doctrine itself is not bad rhetoric. While the Doctrine does read: "The United States will keep all of its treaty commitments," it is unlikely that a president would say that our country won't keep its treaty commitments. This is something that even a president with a much more liberal background than Nixon would say. "We shall provide a shield if a nuclear power threatens the freedom of a nation allied with us or a nation whose survival we consider vital to our security and the security of the region as a whole." And finally, "in cases involving other types of aggression, we shall furnish military and economic assistance when requested and as appropriate." When you add all of these pieces together, it is moving in the direction of a much lower American profile. How far it will move in that direction, we don't know. What the Nixon administration will do at critical moments in Vietnam or Thailand or Korea or Japan, we don't know. But I would say right now the signs appear fairly favorable.

Let's focus for a moment on what we don't know. We don't know much about the meaning of the Nixon Doctrine because its intellectual origins are diverse and obscure—they may be a combination of John Foster Dulles and Morton Halperin. And when one puts those pieces together one wonders about the different things the Nixon Doctrine, and the steps to reduce the United States presence in Asia, could mean. I think it could mean three things. First, it could mean the point that has been made since 1950 in connection with all U. S. military assistance abroad: namely, that our allies ought to be more self-reliant. This doesn't answer any other questions; it just asserts that we want them to be more self-reliant. Second, it could even mean greater reliance on nuclear weapons or a modern version of massive retaliation, which is rather massive deterrence plus reliance on air and sea power for immaculate defense. Or third, it could mean that we really do not ever intend to get involved in another Asian land war of whatever variety.

Let's entertain all these possibilities for a moment, because

there are elements in our government which buy each approach. Which approach Nixon himself buys is very hard to
say. On the first point, self-reliance, Secretary Rogers on September 11, 1970, testified before the Foreign Operations Subcommittee of the Senate Appropriations Committee on the re-
organization of the executive branch for military and
economic assistance. He said the following:

> At the time when this Administration through the Nixon
> Doctrine is encouraging more self-reliance on the part of
> other nations, it is particularly important that we not with-
> draw or even appear to withdraw from our role in the world.
> We are deliberately lowering our military presence in the be-
> lief that Asian countries are increasingly in a position to un-
> dertake their own defense in all but major contingencies. The
> Nixon Doctrine, however, is not a program for U. S. with-
> drawal from Asia. It is a program of readjustment which
> may well mean increased military supplies and increased eco-
> nomic relationships.

So this notion of where the Nixon policy is heading is simply
more self-reliance. We really don't know what we would do in
the face of certain kinds of attacks, whether they be overt conventional or paramilitary guerrilla. But we want to give more
money, more economic and military assistance, to the Asian
countries so that the chances of our being needed in the event
of any of these contingencies would be less. That is one interpretation.

The second interpretation is that the tip-off to the new
Nixon strategy is the change from 2½ contingencies to 1½
contingencies, and that the real meaning of this is that we intend to maintain conventional forces only for Europe and we
really don't intend to have conventional deterrence or defense
in Asia. That is our subtle way, or perhaps not so subtle way,
of telling the Chinese and others that if they commit aggression in the future we will respond with air and sea power and
probably with tactical nuclear weapons. The point of this

would be that (*a*) we ought not to get involved in another Asian land war with American men, but (*b*) our interests in Asia are still sufficiently important to take some military action.

The third interpretation—and this you get less from public statements by various members of the Nixon administration than from newspaper leaks and conversations—is that all the above is the rhetoric which the Nixon administration has to employ but that they are really doing what you want them to do—disengage. They can't say it because the exigencies of diplomacy are such that a government acting responsibly just can't say those things. It would cause panic to make a transition too rapidly. But after all, the Nixon administration is composed of politicians who realize the country is opposed to maintaining the kind of policy for the seventies that it had in the sixties. The public mood is quite contrary to involvement in any wars in Asia. The public does not want any more Vietnams.

I think you can make a case for any of these three interpretations.

There is another problem involved here in the meaning of the Nixon Doctrine. How do we insure that when threats emerge in the future the United States is going to do the things we would like it to do? One hears different notions of what will trigger or allow a lower posture in Asia. One was presented by Secretary of Defense Laird about February 1970. It hasn't been repeated since, but it is in the record. He said the implementation of the Nixon Doctrine depends upon the success of Vietnamization: that is, if Vietnamization works, then the Nixon Doctrine can work. If, by means of our slowly moving out of Vietnam and providing more military and economic assistance to the South Vietnamese, they show they can act against their threat, then we would have the confidence to try a similar approach throughout Asia. The implication is that we may not try it in the rest of Asia unless it works in Vietnam. The assumption remains that our interests in the area are vital and we have to figure out some way of maintaining them. Vietnam is the test case.

A second interpretation of what will allow a lower profile —no Asian land wars—is a remark by Secretary Rogers to the effect that it really doesn't depend so much on the success of Vietnamization, but that it depends on whether or not our country is prepared to provide a substitute for U. S. military presence. And the kind of substitute he talks about in his presentation to the Congress, the kind of substitute that will be more and more emphasized by the Nixon administration, is a massive amount of military and economic assistance.

We received a picture of just how much is involved from leaks in connection with U. S. troop withdrawals from Korea. The Koreans said: we don't want you to get out, but if you are going to withdraw even 20,000 troops you have to help modernize the Korean army; if you really are interested in self-reliance you have to pay for it, and that is going to involve several billion dollars over a five-year period. It means aircraft; it means new tanks, new guns; more ammunition so we can sustain combat. Again the implication is that unless the Congress comes up with the money to provide a substitute for the U. S. presence, we really don't know what we are going to do, because we want to maintain our interest in the area. The trigger is money as a substitute for manpower.

The third interpretation is that none of this matters: not the success of Vietnamization and not money to replace men, because disengagement is going to happen anyway. This is the way the country is trending. President Nixon is a politician; he wants to get reelected; he has to lower the defense budget. There are people in his administration who are determined to see the Republican Party become a majority party again and they realize that they have to avoid U. S. entanglement abroad, so they are going to be pushing in that direction. We should not fight our allies, even if we have to make our rhetoric more hawkish in order to give them confidence in what we are doing. So the greatest danger, according to this view, is that by not trusting an administration we force it to do and say things that it otherwise wouldn't do or say. So keep quiet, we are told, and help develop a new consensus about the Nixon Doctrine and go forward in a sensible, responsible manner.

I have my own hunches about the meaning of the Nixon Doctrine and what would be required for its implementation, but they are only hunches. I don't think any of us knows with confidence what President Nixon believes. We may know what different elements of the government believe, but I don't know how much this counts.

My third point is that regardless of whose interpretation is correct, I think our role must essentially be a critical one. I am reminded of a story about British diplomacy in the nineteenth century. Disraeli was asked to comment on Gladstone's foreign policy, and he said, "Well, if he had one, I would criticize it." I think people could say the same thing about U. S. policy in the sixties and the seventies, despite the very vivid articulation of those policies—despite the appearance that they have been laid out with a great deal of rigor and clarity. We still don't know what they will mean. It depends so much on the man who is president, on how he sees his personal role, the interests of the country, and the domestic politics of the country, and on how he visualizes threats.

The matter of threats is very important. Soviet and Chinese motives and decision-making processes are obscure. Because of this obscurity and uncertainty, these threats can't be dismissed out of hand. Despite this, I would want to lower the defense budget a great deal. But we must do it in a manner that still enables us to meet threats and to give the president responsible choices. Take, for example, the Middle East situation. Many people have dual feelings about Vietnam and the Middle East. I for one feel we ought to set a time limit for Vietnam; it ought to be early and we ought to get out. In the case of the Middle East, however, I believe the history of the situation and our country's attachments to the state of Israel demand some sort of U. S. military assistance in order to insure that the Israelis will be able to defend themselves. I believe what the Soviet Union has been doing there is potentially dangerous. We must maintain capabilities in the event that terrible situations come about that we don't contemplate now, that seem very unlikely now. They always seem unlikely before they materialize.

It sounds like a conservative and discredited argument to say that even though threats are remote, we should plan for them, but I still believe that. We must do it, however, in another way, with less emphasis on sophisticated modern weaponry and more emphasis on maintaining conventional fighting power. The existence of a large conventional force structure—the existence of aircraft carriers, twenty-three air wings, etc.—is not going to push us into a situation when we otherwise would not have been involved. I don't think it has in the past. The critical factor in whether or not the U. S. intervenes militarily is the president of the United States and what he believes.

What we on the outside have to do is insure that the present debate is maintained so that the president and his administration have to justify whatever they do, so that pressures are maintained to push them where we feel they ought to go.

Reactions
from Japan

MORTON H. HALPERIN: The Japanese are very confused about the Nixon Doctrine, the Guam Doctrine, how the
two relate to each other, and what the notion of Vietnamization means. They take it all very seriously. I suspect that more
copies of President Nixon's first State of the World message
have been analyzed in Japan than any other place in the
world, including the United States. The Japanese can tell you
the difference between the Guam Doctrine and the Nixon
Doctrine as stated in his message to Congress in great detail.

I used to tell my Japanese friends before Cambodia that
what we meant when we said we had learned a lesson in Vietnam was that we should not get involved on the Asian mainland in former French colonies, and that was all. It turns out
we haven't even learned that. The Japanese are puzzled. And
because they are puzzled and because they take what we say
seriously, they are in a state of nervousness which is revealed
in a number of ways.

There was an enormous reaction in Japan to President
Johnson's March 31, 1968 speech, which the Japanese
thought meant we were getting out of Asia lock, stock, and
barrel very quickly. Great tremors of nervousness went
through Japan, until they were convinced it was a speech for
domestic consumption and not a speech about American policy in Asia. They also were very upset by the Soviet invasion

of Czechoslovakia; there was more impact in Japan from that invasion than from any other event.

That provides a clue to the small number of things that the Japanese care about in analyzing our Asia policy. The first of these is protection of Japan from the Soviet Union. The Japanese view the Soviets as the only serious threat to their security and are not worried about the Chinese. They need to be convinced that our policies toward the Russians and our reduction in defense expenditures do not mean we will discontinue nuclear protection of Japan against the Soviet Union. For example, they are not terribly impressed that we are building an ABM against China and can therefore protect them, because they are worried about Russian nuclear power rather than Chinese. We should deal with these Japanese attitudes simply by avoiding the extremes that we would avoid in any case for a variety of other reasons: either a very aggressive policy toward the Soviet Union, which would lead the Japanese to believe we may get into a war in which they will be involved; or, on the other hand, unilateral disarmament. But we would have to go quite far in either of those directions to disturb Japan.

As far as Asia is concerned, there are several things the Japanese are concerned about. First, a total American withdrawal from Japan. The Japanese would like very much to reduce our involvement there. But if we went to them tomorrow and said we will have everything out of here in four months, you would see very quickly a major Japanese rearmament and a Japanese nuclear program. The Japanese would also be disturbed, although somewhat less, by a total American withdrawal from Korea. They recognize that the Koreans don't want to be defended by them. On the other hand, they are concerned about North Korea's intentions, not China's, and would be disturbed by a total American withdrawal from Korea.

They would also be disturbed by anything that smacks of an American deal to give Taiwan to China. They would not be upset, however, by a Taiwanese arrangement with the mainland, whatever that meant. And they would not be concerned about anything else we might do to improve our relations with China. But they would be bothered by a cynical deal. I cite these things not because I think any of them likely but only to suggest that extreme instances of U. S. disengagement would seriously trouble the Japanese.

What will concern them most in the question of their future rearmament, nuclear capability, and attitude toward us is the nature of our bilateral relationship to Japan. The fundamental question is whether they feel they are being treated as an equal or as a client. This is partly psychological and partly a matter of consultation—taking their view seriously on issues that are critical to them. But the fundamental question is whether Japan feels it is being treated as a great power, not whether we continue to maintain forces in Thailand, or whether we have 50,000 or 20,000 men in Korea, or whether we build an ABM.

As far as Southeast Asia is concerned, the Japanese interest is quite minimal. The Japanese have discovered that they can trade with countries whether they profess to be western, neutral, or communist. If large numbers of Chinese divisions marched into Southeast Asia, moving inexorably toward Singapore, the Japanese would be concerned. However, such an event is so unlikely that we should not base any policy on a Japanese reaction to it. Anything short of that in Southeast Asia would not have any profound effect on Japan unless the Japanese considered it a symbol for the fact that the United States was about to do the other things I have suggested. But as far as Vietnam is concerned, we have stayed long enough and moved out slowly enough, so that no matter how fast we get out the rest of the way the impact on Japan will be minimal.

At the other extreme, if there is a massive escalation of American involvement in Vietnam—if we return to the notion that the way to end the war is to destroy the North—then there could be profound repercussions in Japan. They would question not our will and determination but our sense of balance and our judgment.

WILLIAM W. WHITSON: I want to comment on Morton Halperin's statement that the Japanese are worried exclusively about the Russians. This is certainly historically true and was true even up to 1969, but it is now changing. While they are now de-emphasizing the Soviet threat, they are building up the Chinese threat. They are now talking about a nuclear China, and the Russians are becoming slightly less important to them. This seems to be a trend that could have its origins in Japanese domestic policy rather than in a conception of real threat. I am not talking about Defense Minister Nakasone alone. What I mean is this: is it perhaps useful to the Japanese suddenly to come around to our view, for their own purposes? While there has certainly been a long-term historical Japanese concern for Russian power in Northeast Asia, this could now be shifting, for a variety of reasons.

DANIEL ELLSBERG: What are the Japanese concerned about from China?

WILLIAM W. WHITSON: The Japanese are concerned first about the direct nuclear threat from the Chinese and what is going to be done about it. Must they do it alone? Is there going to be an American nuclear umbrella? Then, in Southeast Asia, quite apart from Chinese military capability, there is the political and psychological implication of the Chinese threat for the nations there that are Japanese trading partners. And in Taiwan, and elsewhere, they are beginning to see the Chinese role backed up by a nuclear capability. Japanese interests in Asia are probably more immediately threatened by this than by the Russian role.

JOHN W. DOWER: The other side of this coin is that China is becoming increasingly alarmed about military developments in Japan. China is expressing considerable concern about Japanese imperialism and military development. We tend to underestimate Japan's present military capabilities. So there is a great concern on the other side also. And there is the question of Japan going nuclear, which is a very delicate political question. On Peking's list of enemies, Japan is now clearly number one.

EARL C. RAVENAL: Some people might even go beyond William Whitson's comment about changing Japanese estimates of threats and interests, and note that the Japanese and the Soviets together appear to be discovering many common interests in East Asia. Japan and the Soviet Union seem to be converging on a perceived interest in balancing China. They also are being drawn into cooperation in economic activity in Eastern Siberia. This could become the basis for a coordination of Japanese and Soviet policy in that region.

STANLEY M. KANAROWSKI: Another way of making the point is to say that the Soviet Union might adopt a "West German" policy toward Japan and take the initiative with Japan in opening up more trade.

JOHN W. DOWER: At the time Dulles negotiated the Security Treaty with Japan, there were two alleged threats to Japan. One was the Soviet Union and the other was China. But it is my impression that the Japanese accepted neither as a really valid threat. Japan did not see either country as posing a threat to Japan which would necessitate American bases there. This was rather the Dulles notion. I don't deny the fear and animosity people like Prime Minister Yoshida had toward Russia in 1950. But he did not agree with Dulles. The Security Treaty was very much forced on the Japanese; it was the price they had to pay for getting a peace treaty.

WILLIAM W. WHITSON: My point was not simply a shift in Japanese perception but rather a long-term tendency of American practice. The United States tries to impose its perception of threats on its allies in Asia or elsewhere in the world, rather than trying to find out how *they* perceive threats. We build force structures and bases on our perception of these threats, and then try to sell this perception to our clients. We come up with some very strange situations in Thailand and elsewhere, where we sell so hard that they finally say, "Give us the money and we will go ahead and play your game."

Will the Nixon Doctrine
Mean Anything?

ROBERT E. OSGOOD: The changed estimate of the threat, with respect to China and other states, is the single most important change that has taken place in American policy in Asia. If that changed estimate happens to correspond with events, with trends in international politics, then the Nixon Doctrine will mean a great deal. If it doesn't, it won't.

Let me explain what I mean. No doctrine, no general policy statement like the Nixon Doctrine, can be remotely like a blueprint, can even be a policy guideline in any specific sense. It is bound to be ambiguous—even deliberately ambiguous. A problem would occur if you were too specific in saying what you won't do. You might, for example, undermine the deterrent effect on some and raise unwarranted apprehensions in others.

The Nixon Doctrine indicates an intended direction of policy, and that intended direction is toward more selective involvement, not toward a massive withdrawal or a generalized withdrawal. It is interesting historically that among all the various doctrines that the United States has promulgated, this is the only one that explicitly indicates a direction toward limitation and restraint. The Monroe Doctrine, the Truman Doctrine were quite the opposite.

Each doctrine has had a life of its own, determined by events and reinterpretations. In trying to decide what the

Nixon Doctrine might mean, you have to come to grips with the fact that it reflects certain precedents in recommending restraints upon American policy. The avoidance of land war in Asia, the encouragement of self-reliance, especially regional self-reliance, and other historical elements of American policy are echoed in the Nixon Doctrine. This is one of the oldest themes of American policy, that we are not going to do the whole job ourselves. We are not going to be the world's gendarme, as Secretary Rusk and others repeatedly said. This theme goes back to before World War II. And yet our history since World War II has been one of continual extensions of American power, of American involvement, and of American definition of its interests in the world, including its vital interests. So you can't rely upon history to confirm with any assurance that the Doctrine itself will be carried out in practice, because there has been this continual contradiction throughout American policy, between the intention to remain as disengaged as possible and the actual extension of American involvement. Of course, by the same token, this doesn't prove that the same thing will happen in the future.

In order to understand this phenomenon, you have to ask why history has continually refuted intentions. Obviously, in this case it has to do primarily with the strength of the strategy of containment and of the Truman Doctrine. I shan't explain the appeal of the strategy of containment or the Truman Doctrine. I will just take it for granted here. It also has to do with the structure of power in the world which existed after World War II and has existed through much of the post-World War II era. So that when a perceived threat of the extension of communist control, especially by violent means, occurred, the counsel of containment and the Truman Doctrine overruled whatever reluctance there might have been to become further involved. Under the circumstances, and especially considering the short run effects, this seemed to be the less objectionable alternative. You don't need to assume any special domestic political expediency to explain that response to a set of unanticipated circumstances. It's the most common thing in the history of great powers. It has to do with pride of power, with consciousness of the symbolic role of power, even in circumstances where vital interests are not immediately engaged, and with the whole approach to power and national interests that great powers have always manifested. It's analogous in a way to empires, even though we are not literally speaking of an American empire. Of course presidents don't like to be in office when they meet with reversal, especially if they are identified with the humiliation of the state. That shouldn't be especially puzzling to historians. But the ethos that has driven the United States to intervene—even when presidents have been advised on a cost-accounting basis that we were going to get into a lot of trouble if we extended our involvement—is understandable in much simpler and yet more profound terms than political expediency.

The real question is: Have we any reason to think that in the future the situation will be any different? Have we any reason to think that the Nixon Doctrine will not be refuted by history and by unanticipated events? I think there are several reasons why we might reach that conclusion, though they are not definitive. One reason to think that the Nixon Doctrine might be carried out in practice, and that the situation in the future is not going to be the one that has characterized the extension of American commitments throughout the Cold War, is simply the extent of the trauma of the Vietnam war, which is qualitatively different from the trauma of the Korean involvement. In both cases, there is a "never again" spirit, but the reaction to Korea led to the *extension* of containment by what were thought to be safer and cheaper means (that is, deterrent alliances), not to a challenge to the premises of American policy upon which we intervened, whereas the reaction to the Vietnam war has led to the beginning of a reassessment of these premises. It has not, I am quick to add, led to an overthrowing of the general policy of containment, and I don't think it should in any wholesale fashion. But it has led to a significant reassessment of some of the bases of American policy pertaining to the implementation of containment, and this did not occur after the Korean War.

Another reason to think that the Nixon Doctrine might mean more than history would lead one to think is simply that retrenchment is actually taking place in Asia (for example, in South Korea and Okinawa) as well as in other parts of the world. So it isn't just rhetoric, though that in itself doesn't prove that the Nixon Doctrine will really mean something.

Another factor is the shrinkage of U. S. capabilities, especially general purpose forces available for Third World intervention. Just as the expansion of U. S. capabilities has led to the expansion of America's definition of its interests and the multiplication of its options, especially when it comes to using American forces against a threat of communist aggression, the constriction of American capabilities may have the opposite effect. Now, one might say that would only mean that, if the threat is held constant, we become more dependent upon tactical nuclear weapons. But I think this is not the case, because a great deal has happened in our view of the utility of tactical nuclear weapons since 1954 and 1958–1959. It's an entirely different situation now. The inhibitions against using tactical nuclear weapons are now much greater. And quite apart from those inhibitions, we have a much lower estimate of their practical utility in the contingencies that are likely to arise.

Another factor that has changed that would lead one to think that the Nixon Doctrine might mean something is that we have, as a result of the Vietnam war, a quite different estimate than we had as we were getting more deeply into it, of the efficacy of America's military power in dealing with that kind of situation, which is an internal and an external war combined. It's a very skeptical estimate, even among the military—perhaps especially among the military—who have been involved in it. But I wouldn't overdo that factor either. None of these factors by itself warrants any confident predictions about what the Nixon Doctrine will mean.

Another factor is domestic constraints, which qualitatively are now different from any other period since World War II. There is a competition between domestic expenditures and external military expenditures that has not existed before.

Now all this doesn't prove what is going to happen in the future. These are simply indicators. If there is a new threat of a communist takeover—and every new threat seems unlike the last one, so it wouldn't be either a Korean type or a Vietnamese type—then I would expect that the United States would still react according to the strategy of containment. All you can say is that the United States would assess that particular situation very carefully, and not automatically, as a kind of conditioned reflex from the familiar set of assumptions about the world and America's power. It would have a much harder look, and it would judge the situation in a much more complicated and ad hoc way.

So far as that part of the Nixon Doctrine which depends upon an increase in self-reliance on the part of others is concerned, this is surely a forlorn hope insofar as it envisages other states, like Japan, taking over America's security role. There are no signs of this development. But the decisive question in predicting the future of the Nixon Doctrine is really: what is the nature of the threat—and "threat" means many different things. If there is going to be a series of communist aggressions, especially aggressions in which China is implicated, then you would reach one set of conclusions; but if not, you would reach quite a different set of conclusions. My conclusion is that the Nixon Doctrine is really a gamble that the threat of communist aggression is much less than the commonly expressed official view in the previous three administrations.

I was struck, upon reading various documents in the government, by the extent to which this altered estimate of the threat is integral to the government's own analysis of one situation after another. It is integral to a quite different assumption about the nature of the Third World than one heard voiced during the Kennedy period. There is quite a different analysis of China, in particular. The government's analysis has come much closer to that of the sinologists. It has accepted and acted upon an analysis that emerged in the intelligence community before the Nixon administration. The whole question of the circumstances under which it would be wise or feasible for the United States to intervene in an internal war is now looked at in a much different way than you would suppose if all you were looking at was the public rhetoric of spokesmen of past administrations. There is a different estimate of the nature of the communist world, the Third World, and particularly the Asian world; and that is a significant fact.

So the decisive question is: what is the nature of the world going to be like? Is the nature of international politics in Asia going to confirm this different analysis of the threat or isn't it? Because there has not been any great systematic change in our estimate of American interests or even in the strategy of containment. What there has been is a different estimate of the efficacy of American power under some kinds of circumstances, and most of all a different estimate of the nature of the threat to America's interests. This is the decisive variable.

I won't try to predict what the Asian environment is going to be like over the next twenty years. Let me simply say what it would have to be like in order to confirm this changed estimate of the threat, and thereby enable the Nixon Doctrine to mean a great deal. It would presume the early liquidation of American combat involvement in Vietnam, and of course that is a very big "if." It would presume that Thailand, Malaysia, and Singapore survive as fairly viable states. It does not necessarily presuppose that Laos or Cambodia or even Vietnam itself would be bastions of stability or even full-fledged states. Those areas are rather more likely to return to their pre-colonial states of affairs, in any case. It does presuppose some kind of growing interregional cooperation—not the creation of a vast Asian alliance or of any highly organized military cooperation, but the emergence of a whole network of economic, diplomatic and military staff relationships at least, which would be politically significant. It also presupposes that Japan will become a more important element in the Asian balance of power, perhaps by coming to have a special interest in the security of Taiwan and Korea as the United States phases out. It presupposes a continued devaluation of our interest in Taiwan. And it presupposes the emergence of a kind of multipolar balance of power in Asia—though not in the nineteenth century sense of the word—a multipolar balance of power within which China finds an interest in operating in a more normal diplomatic way, much as the Soviet Union does, rather than conceiving of its interests entirely as polarized against the United States and as an active leader of revolutions, which is not likely to be a very promising line for China in any case.

If these circumstances were to come about, then it would be quite likely that the U. S. presence in Asia would be reduced. And it is that very reduction of the American presence that would lead to a reduction of our estimate of our interests in Asia, since this would be analogous to the divesting of the imperial responsibilities that we have acquired. If all that takes place, then you will be able to look back on the Nixon Doctrine, without giving any special credit to anyone, twenty-five or thirty-five years from now, and say: this was a decisive turning point, and the president who happened to be in office at that point had the wit to state it in rather ambiguous words which nevertheless came to have a life of their own—just as the Truman Doctrine did, but in quite a different direction. If, however, events and conditions are quite different from the ones I pose, then long before twenty-five years you will look at the Nixon Doctrine as a kind of fraud. That would be unfair, but history is not always kind—even to American presidents.

The Hidden Significance
of the Nixon Doctrine

JOHN W. DOWER: Since the summer of 1969, the U. S. government has placed increasing emphasis upon its alleged adoption of a new policy toward Asia. First suggested by the president in July 1969 at an informal press conference on Guam, the Nixon Doctrine is generally and correctly associated with the projected partial "disengagement" of American combat forces from Asia. This includes not only proposed troop withdrawals from Vietnam, but also from American bases elsewhere in Asia. Thus a reduction of the substantial American garrison which has been maintained in Korea since the Korean War was announced. The November 1969 Sato-Nixon communiqué calling for return of Okinawa to Japanese rule by 1972 is generally described as part of the Nixon Doctrine, and it is anticipated that during the 1970s the Japanese military will gradually take over many functions now carried out by U. S. servicemen in both Okinawa and Japan proper. The Thai government announced that it expects the number of American soldiers stationed in Thailand to be reduced "after" the present Indochina conflict. And so on. The essential ingredient in the new "low posture" or "low profile," in short, is that the most visible American presence in Asia—its combat troops there (in 1970 still close to 1 million in number)—will be reduced.

The other side of the Nixon Doctrine is Asian self-help. In

President Nixon's phrase, "Asian hands must shape the Asian future." More specifically, pro-American Asian regimes are to be strengthened militarily so that in the suppression of future "insurgencies" they can shoulder a major part of the burden borne up to now by the U. S. At the same time, the United States will stand by with its nuclear arsenal and tactical support, honoring its commitments and vigilant against external aggression. In Nixon's words:

> First, the United States will keep all of its treaty commitments.
>
> Second, we shall provide a shield if a nuclear power threatens the freedom of a nation allied with us, or of a nation whose survival we consider vital to our security.
>
> Third, in cases involving other types of aggression we shall furnish military and economic assistance when requested in accordance with our treaty commitments. But we shall look to the nation directly threatened to assume the primary responsibility of providing the manpower for its defense.

While the primary thrust of the doctrine is military, the economic side is not ignored. Here President Nixon stresses interregional cooperation—"Asian initiatives in an Asian framework"—abetted by "multinational" corporations and organizations. At the same time, however, it is acknowledged that in both military and economic matters, "Japan's partnership with us will be a key to the success of the Nixon Doctrine in Asia."

Since the present situation is tragic, the future uncertain, and some of the sentiments of the Nixon Doctrine rather admirable on the surface, it is generally regarded as uncharitable to speak harshly of President Nixon's vision of the future relationship between the United States and Asia. Still it might be of some help in looking to that future to keep the following considerations in mind:

1. The Nixon Doctrine is not new. Rather, like many of Nixon's basic views, it can be traced back to the early years of

the cold war and particularly the Dulles policy of "letting
Asians fight Asians." Also, nothing in Nixon's various formulations of the Doctrine (notably on July 25 and November 3,
1969, and January 22 and February 18, 1970) would have
been rejected by the policy makers (including Nixon himself
in the early 1950s) who encouraged and planned the American intervention in Indochina over the past decades. Following the "State of the World" message of February 18, 1970, for
example, Max Frankel of *The New York Times* noted that
"Mr. Nixon's aides concede . . . that there is nothing in his
new doctrine that excludes a Dominican-style intervention in
defense of vital interests. They say that the document is a call
to the nation and Government to define those interests more
precisely and prudently than in the past, but they have only
begun that job and it is never really finished until the moment
of crisis."

2. The basic analysis of the situation in Asia and of
America's proper relation to it has not changed. On the one
hand, "We remain involved in Asia. We are a Pacific power." In
his October 1967 *Foreign Affairs* article, Nixon argues that
"both our interests and our ideals propel us westward across
the Pacific"—a sentiment which can be traced back to the
American expansionists of 1898 and the vision of Asia as the
"new Far West." On the other hand, the goals of containing
China, checking "communism," suppressing "insurgencies,"
and continuing to support pro-American Asian regimes, however corrupt, remain.

In his first State of the World message, President Nixon did
acknowledge that nationalism had proven itself destructive of
"international Communist unity," and he also called for "improved practical relations with Peking." In the same breath,
however, he reaffirmed America's military commitment to the
Nationalist regime in Taiwan, and reiterated the familiar con-
descending hope that "sooner or later communist China will
be ready to re-enter the international community." There is no
indication that, despite the ongoing American bloodbath in

Indochina and the restraint China has demonstrated in the face of this, President Nixon has revised his view that China still poses a great threat in Asia today. Both the military and the State Department have faithfully reiterated this same point; on July 9, 1970, for example, scarcely two months after the U. S. invasion of Cambodia, Secretary of State William P. Rogers appeared on a television interview in Tokyo and blandly urged China to abandon its "belligerent attitude" toward the world and play "a sensible role in the international community."

In a similar manner, the new official version of polycentric communism has not prevented Nixon from reviving and reemphasizing the domino theory (most notably in his television interview of July 2, 1970), or the Pentagon from viewing the objective in Asia as "the development of good land forces capable of offering a credible deterrent to a Communist aggression." Perhaps of even greater significance, neither the political and social, as well as military, viability of the National Liberation Front (NLF) and Pathet Lao—nor the sharply contrasting corruption and inefficiency of the regimes the U. S. supports against them—has caused the government to reconsider its attitude of total opposition to popular revolutionary movements in Asia. This, in fact, remains a bedrock of the Nixon Doctrine. In Secretary of Defense Melvin Laird's words:

> The principal threat to the independent nations in Asia is internal insurgency, supported by external assistance. This is an important aspect of the threat to which our General Purpose Force planning for Asia should be oriented.

In the future as in the past (as seen in the case of China as well as Indochina) it can be anticipated that American officials will continue to place unwarranted emphasis on the role of "external assistance" while minimizing more relevant and determining indigenous developments. But the fundamental American objective in Asia remains—as has been the case since before the Second World War—containment and counter-revolution.

3. The Nixon Doctrine is fundamentally a cost-conscious policy, aimed at maintaining a major U. S. role in Asia at less cost in both dollars and American lives. This emerges vividly in Ambassador Bunker's statement that Vietnamization simply means changing the color of the corpses. In a similar manner, former Defense Secretary Clark Clifford informed Congress in January 1969 that "an Asian soldier costs about $\frac{1}{15}$ as much as his American counterpart," and Secretary Laird argued for an expanded Military Assistance Program (MAP), mostly for Asia, on the grounds that "a MAP dollar is of far greater value than a dollar spent directly on U. S. forces." One key benefit of a substantial withdrawal of manpower from Asia will be that this could permit reduction of the defense budget and provide a substantial check on the "dollar drain." One consequence of attempting to maintain the old objectives and commitments on the cheap may well be to increase the likelihood of a resort to tactical nuclear weapons.

4. The plan to withdraw American troops is itself a qualified one. In the first place, the emphasis is on ground combat troops, while support forces, particularly aviation units, are being retained to a large extent. In addition, there is no reason to believe that anything other than a "Korean solution" is being considered for Vietnam—that is, that withdrawals will not continue after a certain level of remaining troops, possibly in the 100,000 area, is reached. Furthermore, the U. S. government has given no clear indication of which of its several hundred major bases in Asia it intends to relinquish. While some may indeed be phased out as obsolete or uneconomical, there is no intention of abandoning the "ring of steel" around China.

5. Client armies are to assume some of the functions now carried out by the U. S. military. "Vietnamization"—the corrupt, brutalizing policy by which the South Vietnamese army is now supposedly assuming increased military responsibility

—is cited as a model of the Nixon Doctrine in action. So also is the deployment of South Vietnamese (ARVN) and Thai troops in an essentially mercenary capacity in Cambodia—to prop up a regime which is acknowledged to lack popular support. Despite the fact that the one-million-man ARVN has been in the making for over a decade and still cannot hold its own without decisive American air and combat support against numerically and technologically inferior NLF and North Vietnamese forces, this appears to be the path of the future for America's Asian allies: more U. S. military aid (note the accelerating commitment to the Lon Nol regime in Cambodia); more U. S. military advisers (witness the new John F. Kennedy Center for Military Assistance at Fort Bragg); more military training for Asian nationals (Thai soldiers, for example, are already receiving CBW (chemical and biological warfare) training in the U. S. in preparation for the day when they too can participate in the defoliation of their land); a larger policy-making role for the Pentagon and CIA (witness the recent proposal to turn AID functions over to the Pentagon); emphasis upon police functions and control mechanisms within the society (close to 50 percent of the "civilian" aid budget to Thailand is now being spent on police stations and specially trained Special Police); and so on. In effect, the U. S. seeks to defend its ambitions in Asia through proxy armies and client regimes.

6. American military planners also anticipate that much of the slack of disengagement will be taken up by major technological advances in warfare. These include the transportation revolution represented by the C-5A super transport—an innovation which to a considerable extent makes the need for an intricate network of overseas forward bases obsolete. In the words of its manufacturer, Lockheed:

The C-5A Galaxy is more than the world's largest airplane. It's a new kind of defense system. It's like having a military base in nearly every strategic spot on the globe.

To the new concept of rapid deployment must be added the Westmoreland dream of the electronic battlefield. This too, it is anticipated, will greatly lessen the manpower requirements of future "counterinsurgency" situations—if it works. As Westmoreland describes it, "With surveillance devices that can continually track the enemy, the need for large forces to fix the opposition physically will be less important." Even without a "Nixon Doctrine," the logic of military technology would have dictated a gradual "disengagement" of manpower from Asia.

7. The combination of old objectives, cost-consciousness, and reluctance to become mired in another land war in Asia increases the possibility of resort to nuclear weapons in the future. As vice president, Nixon himself publicly declared in 1955:

> It is foolish to talk about the possibility that the weapons which might be used in the event war breaks out in the Pacific would be limited to the conventional Korean and World War II types of explosives. Our forces could not fight an effective war in the Pacific with those types of explosives if they wanted to. Tactical atomic explosives are now conventional and will be used against the military targets of any aggressive force.

A policy of defending one's commitments by withdrawing and relying upon disreputable client armies and unperfected battlefield electronics is a shaky one at best, and very likely to find itself challenged. Neither Nixon's past attitude toward nuclear weapons, his pledges to take decisive action in Indochina if challenged (for example, May 8, 1970), his reliance upon advisers known to be especially tolerant of using tactical nuclear weapons in certain situations, nor his personal propensity for equating virility with destruction dispel this concern.

8. In the economic realm, the Nixon Doctrine offers no real alternative to policies already discredited. The rubric of "multinationalism" cannot cover the fact that the future economic development projected by the Doctrine is to take place

within a capitalist system dominated by the United States and Japan, with a high probability that the underdeveloped countries of Asia—as has been the case in Latin America—will be locked into a state of permanent dependence. The problems of foreign investment and foreign aid are not faced squarely by the Nixon Doctrine, and it remains an unquestioned assumption that capitalism alone can offer hope for a better future to the Third World. In fact, the record suggests that economic domination by the United States and Japan is more likely to create artificial consumer economies for the rich in the midst of rural stagnation and urban decay, or—at best—an economy such as that of South Korea, dominated by Japanese and American corporations, with enormous foreign debts and hopeless corruption. Past examples and present trends, in Latin America as well as Asia itself, suggest that reliance upon "multinational" aid, trade, and investment along the lines Nixon seems to have in mind will create or consolidate native elites more intent upon personal aggrandizement than on public works; will exacerbate rather than resolve existing schisms between city and countryside and between rich and poor; will foster a system of "industrial dualism" in which a favored sector of manufactures is encouraged and protected to the neglect of a far larger sector of native crafts and cottage industries; and will lock the recipient countries into a permanently inferior and dependent relationship with the advanced capitalist countries. For example, two Yale economists, Bell and Resnick, in June 1970 surveyed the results of postwar economic development in the "private enterprise economies" of Southeast Asia and concluded that "in human terms, the result of the last twenty-five years has meant abysmally low levels of consumption, education, health and welfare for about two-thirds of the people."

It should be kept in mind also that as "multinational" stakes in the country increase, the pressure for outside intervention to suppress popular protest and threats to the status quo will also increase.

9. In the political and social realms, the Nixon Doctrine

promises support of the same type of generally corrupt, inefficient, exploitative regimes which the United States has favored
in the past. The focus remains upon attempting to bring about
change through a military or urban elite which—as case after
case has shown—can never carry out thoroughgoing and
meaningful reforms without undermining its own privileged
position. The absurdity of the American claim to be "defending the rights of the people of Southeast Asia" by defending
pro-American regimes against forces within their own societies is evident in the most obvious American contribution to
Indochina today: a moonscape of craters and defoliated for-
ests and devastated rice fields, with millions of refugees rotting
in urban slums and refugee camps. It is evident in the venal
puppet regimes in Saigon and Vientiane. It is evident outside
the theater of war—in the Philippines, for example, where
seven decades of intimate American involvement have produced the "democracy" of the 1969 Philippine elections. As
Tillman Durdin of *The New York Times* reported (November
16, 1969):

> Filipinos view elections as a confirmation of the power of the
> wealthy business and landed interests who back both parties
> but usually pick the winners before Election Day and quietly
> give them the most support. In this case they picked Presi-
> dent Marcos.

Yet once again, the model offered in the Nixon Doctrine ignores the record and ignores as well the dynamic of social and
political change which has thus far proven itself most viable in
underdeveloped, largely peasant societies: change initiated in
the countryside and calling upon the energies of the people
themselves.

10. In the realm of international affairs, the Nixon Doctrine enforces bipolarization. Whatever verbal allegations the
Nixon administration may make to the contrary, the record
clearly indicates that American support invariably goes to
those elements in a country who in external affairs support the

United States and in internal affairs endorse private enterprise and are tolerant of considerable foreign involvement. The result is to polarize forces within the society on the one hand (as seen in South Vietnam), and on the other hand to make adherence to an independent role in diplomacy extremely difficult for nations caught in the path of the American juggernaut (as witness the effect of American actions on Cambodia, Laos, and both North and South Vietnam). The attitude that neutrality is inherently immoral has its roots in the moral globalism of the Dulles period, but whatever its origins, the fact remains that there is a greater degree of national sovereignty and greater independence in foreign affairs within the so-called "communist camp" in Asia than exists among the nations of what Nixon chooses to call "free Asia." The latter remains an alliance heavily reliant upon American aid; greatly indebted to America's postwar military spending and wars in Asia for much of its economic growth; increasingly dependent upon a market system dominated by the United States and Japan; and predominantly judged not by its contribution to the well-being of its peoples, but rather by its anticommunist credentials and its contribution, real or potential, to American military objectives in Asia.

In saying this, there is no intention of denying present trends toward a multipolar configuration in contemporary Asia, with China, the Soviet Union, the United States, and Japan playing the leading power roles. This must, in fact, be a key point of focus in any attempt to comprehend Asia's future, and it would be foolish to assert that the Nixon administration does not recognize this. At best, however, this recognition can only be described as a grudging one, a rather technocratic endeavor to reconcile new power realities in Asia with other changing political, economic, and military considerations—and to do so with the least possible sacrifice of old, often killing, but generally comfortable shibboleths concerning the nature and needs of Asia's peoples and America's proper role toward them. The Nixon Doctrine is good domestic politics, perhaps; it is obviously high time for the low posture at home. It is hardly statesmanship, however, and indeed little more than one would have expected to be tossed up in any case by the normal momentum of time, technology, bureaucracy, and imperial pride.

Never Again?

RICHARD A. FALK: There is a prevailing sense that I find within the policy-making establishment to the effect that the Vietnam war was an exceptional event in recent American foreign policy. There are variations on this basic interpretation: either that it was an exceptional event in that it displayed a disproportionate relationship between valid means and valid ends; or that it was a mistaken and tragic policy because it was so costly, either in its effects on American society or in its failure to achieve the political or military objectives in Southeast Asia for the initially anticipated costs.

The liberal Democratic view, the view of the people in the Kennedy-Johnson administration, is essentially built around this kind of position—not questioning the validity of the ideological and counterrevolutionary posture which was implicit in undertaking to uphold the Saigon regime or even to help impose it on South Vietnam. The principal variation on this view is embodied in the Nixon Doctrine and various formulations that come close to it and represent the moderate Republican Party view: again this position holds that the mission was perfectly valid and indeed desirable, but that there was a political, economic and military mistake made by relying to an unnecessary extent upon American ground forces. The reliance on U. S. ground forces generated intense and unpredictable forms of dissent at home and produced superfluous economic costs. An Asian soldier can be fielded for a fraction of the dollar cost (1/10 to 1/15) of an American soldier.

Therefore, we are confronted with this consensus that says that a Vietnam-type war is a good thing provided you don't carry it too far—that is, in terms of costs—that it is therefore necessary to rely even more on the high-technology military establishment that we have at our disposal, and on our comparative economic and military advantage. One relies on air power. One takes very seriously the threat to use nuclear weapons. And one thinks of the American role as providing the technological backup to carry on the counterrevolutionary mission that the United States has in the Third World and in Southeast Asia in particular. And one describes the process in terms of our interests or of our commitments. One translates counterrevolutionary and establishment rhetoric into the projection and the defense of American interests. This becomes an acceptable kind of euphemism and tends to discourage difficult questions about what our objectives are and what are the real motivations for our policies toward underdeveloped countries.

In other words, within the debate on the Vietnam war itself —and this includes most antiwar critics as well as administration defenders—there is no serious questioning of the underlying premises of the policies that are at stake in Southeast Asia. An example of this essentially conservative consensus is the statement of Les Gelb earlier in this conference. He is now an avowed critic of the Vietnam war, but only a short while ago worked in the Defense Department to carry out President Johnson's war policies, a role that he has never renounced. And he seems just now to have expressed approval of the Nixon policies in Asia.

One hears talk of "never again." There is a tremendous ambiguity in that phrase, to put it charitably. Because "never again" is *already* taking place. We are presently fighting counterinsurgency wars in Cambodia and Laos that have nothing to do with the intention of trying to end the war in Vietnam.

These other Indochinese conflicts are in many respects separate undertakings involving the use of U. S. resources, including logistic capabilities, air power, and other kinds of military
assistance. These support operations are designed to accomplish by different tactics the same result that was sought in
Vietnam.

There is every evidence, as well, that we are continuing to
uphold our so-called commitments to repressive governments
throughout Asia and elsewhere, and to provide those governments with the military means they need to maintain their
control over their national society; in other words, we are
helping these governments turn their own armies into mercenary armies that act as agents for American imperialism
throughout the Third World; we talk of these undertakings in
terms of providing stability for Asia, Latin America, or whatever it is. This kind of commitment pattern assures a continuation of the general drift of American policy. It is also likely
to produce cruel kinds of wars in the future. Whenever counterinsurgency missions rely upon high-technology weaponry, the
effects on the civilian population tend to verge on horror. Indeed, counterinsurgency operations of large scale become gen-
ocidal in their impact upon a society. The weaponry is indis-
criminate in its character, and victory is defined in terms of
destroying the population base upon which a revolutionary
movement rests. Therefore, there is no ground for optimism
that reducing the level of involvement, or even ending the specific involvement itself, in Vietnam will lead to a different
kind of policy, or avoid the same destructive role for American policy in foreign underdeveloped societies.

There is even reason to suppose that the American government is moving toward the adoption of a counterrevolutionary
posture toward dissent at home. Just as foreign policy tends to
be an extension of domestic politics and values, so domestic
policies often import the struggle that was waged abroad. Al-
gerians returned home in 1954 from their conscripted role in
France's counterinsurgency war in Indochina to invert the

training and tactics, and thereby commence the Algerian war of independence. Increasingly, the Defense Department treats domestic dissent as if it were an incipient "Vietcong." There are hard reports, for instance, of Defense Department contracts in which a counterinsurgency design allegedly specified in terms of a foreign city—say, Sao Paulo—is actually specified in terms of an American city—say, Chicago. That is, the Defense Department, spying on domestic politicians of moderate outlook, is orienting itself for a struggle at home along the lines of the one it has been waging these many years in Vietnam.

Instead of maintaining an imperial presence based on counterinsurgency doctrine and weaponry, it would be domestically and internationally beneficial if the United States renounced an independent military role for itself in the Third World. The U. S. government should abandon the projection of its military power into foreign conflicts and limit its security policy to the strict defense of the United States as a territorial entity. In addition it should, in certain circumstances, facilitate United Nations peace-keeping activities. But beyond these limited tasks U. S. military power is likely to have a destructive impact for the world and for ourselves.

MARCUS G. RASKIN: Where is the constituency for your view in the United States? If it is the case that the liberal Democrats basically hold to the framework that we know they hold to, and the conservative or moderate Republicans hold to the framework that we know they hold to, what is the balance of forces within the United States that will produce a foreign policy that can relate to what you are saying?

RICHARD A. FALK: There remains an uncertainty about the degree to which the more progressive elements in the spectrum of political outlook could be converted to my interpretation of what the American role should be in world affairs. A degree of mystification has resulted from the false effort to explain away Vietnam (vindicate, in retrospect, the lost lives and the dreadful internal agony), just as fifteen years earlier there was a similar false effort to explain away Korea as a "never again" involvement of the United States. There is some possibility that an enlightened self-interest perspective, if dramatically enough communicated, would convert to my views a portion of those who are active in organized elective politics. But at the present time the only adherents to the view that I am taking are isolated individuals associated with radical politics and outside the organized channels of political action in the United States. It is very depressing that the national debate does not even include a consideration of the fact that our foreign policy mission itself is wrong throughout the Third World.

LEONARD RODBERG: It is implicit in Marcus Raskin's question that every segment of American society which has made it—that is, from the working class up—has a stake in the present military system. If you want to find a constituency for a new kind of policy, you cannot go to the self-interest of these classes. You must look to those people who are outside of the economy.

RICHARD A. FALK: Unless you regard their presently perceived self-interest as a false rendering of their real self-interest. In my judgment our present policy is very destructive, both economically and politically, for some of the people who endorse it most strongly. By and large, those asserting their Americanism by carrying placards that read "God bless the Establishment" and by championing the war are badly deceived on both an ideological and economic level. It is the working class that is being caught in the inflationary spiral that represents some of the deferred costs of the long and expensive Vietnam involvement.

LESLIE H. GELB: I thought I had made very clear my position on the Nixon Doctrine. I said we do not know what it means; that there are various interpretations that one might give to it; but with the exception of the disastrous situation in Indochina, the Nixon administration is doing roughly the things that any president would do. We don't really know what this rhetoric adds up to; what it might mean in a crunch; whether the United States might get into wars we wouldn't want to get into. My statement was agnostic, not conservative.

How do we know what is in the president's mind? I have my suspicions, but I don't know. It matters a lot, because he is the critical figure in whether the world comes out looking one way or another five years from now—whether or not we get into another land war in Asia or another kind of war.

The last five presidents have done the same thing in Indochina. The reason is that their actions are rooted in the same political system with the same political values, and with the same perspective on foreign affairs—the kind that believes in domino theories and can weave these domino theories into a compelling reality. They can believe, as John F. Kennedy did in his statement to Kenneth O'Donnell, that they can't take the courageous step of leadership *now* to pull the United States out of Vietnam; they have to wait until after the election. Though some would like to read that statement as showing that Kennedy knew the way out of Vietnam, to others it is a condemnation of the political system: that he felt that even five more lives or even one more life had to be lost in Vietnam in order not to jeopardize his chances for reelection. That is a testimony to the kind of politics that are behind our foreign policy. That is why we must keep up the pressure and the criticism. We can't take the chance that the president is looking at the world the same way we do.

RICHARD A. FALK: It is true, as you emphasize, that we don't yet know enough to assess fully the Nixon Doctrine. But in the sense of whether there is a renunciation of the specific counterinsurgency pledge in Indochina or elsewhere, the Nixon Doctrine is quite evident in its intention and in the early phases of its execution. President Nixon has demonstrated by now—by territorial escalation of the war and by his disinclination to negotiate a compromise ending in Paris —that he is prepared to prolong the fighting indefinitely and to incur grave risks in search for a result that resembles "victory," that is, the maintenance in power of an anticommunist regime in Saigon. You appear to accept the basic framework as inevitable.

LESLIE H. GELB: Nothing is inevitable.

RICHARD A. FALK: You said that any president in his position would have said about the same thing.

LESLIE H. GELB: If he got elected in the United States.

RICHARD A. FALK: But such an assertion supports my principal point. We are decisively enveloped as a nation in a set of foreign policy directives that are highly destructive to ourselves and catastrophic to those societies that have experienced their impacts. We know fully enough about that. What we don't know is how the government will specifically respond to a revolutionary movement at a particular flash point. But I regard this degree of uncertainty as much more marginal than you evidently do. There always exists an area of uncertainty in relation to any broad doctrine of foreign policy. But the basic logic of past policies is clearly being carried forward intact from the past. The Nixon Doctrine maintains the continuity of American involvement and intervention in the Third World, and particularly in Asia.

LESLIE H. GELB: I think you are making a good point. But if you are right and the basic problem is the substructure of our society, economic and political—that what we do in the world must inevitably be anticommunist—then we never would have let any country go communist that we could have prevented from going communist. That would mean that we would have intervened in China in 1948.

RICHARD A. FALK: We did involve ourselves to some extent, but we were not yet psychologically or ideologically prepared for a full-scale counterinsurgency role in 1948. Besides, the pattern of commitment does not entail the sort of absolutism your comment implies. There might be a variety of other considerations, including the apparent magnitude of the task, that could discourage a particular counterinsurgent undertaking without invalidating the basic rule that the United States lends support to counterrevolutionary causes throughout the Third World.

LESLIE H. GELB: But we got out. We didn't go to war. And why didn't we go to war to keep Cuba out of communist hands? Why did we let Castro come in? Because Eisenhower was duped? If he was duped, why didn't he go back with the requisite force? Kennedy tried to, though there was a very low chance of success, as we know in retrospect. Finally, why didn't we get involved in the Nigerian civil war? It is overwhelming the way you characterize the "inevitability" of all of these things. I think there are crucial things wrong with our government and our society that need to be changed. We must criticize them. But none of it is inevitable.

MARCUS G. RASKIN: I don't want to be understood as saying that there is an inevitability to all of this. But there is a sense wherein we have to be much more clear on the meanings of engagement and intervention. You can engage economically. You can engage through the CIA. You can engage militarily. You can engage with military assistance. You can engage through a whole series of undertakings to bring about an end. The fact that you have those particular options does not mean that if you don't use the military one, you are not attempting to control a situation. You can differentiate among types of engagement; but you can't say that because we didn't intervene in X or Y place or in a certain manner, we are not interventionist.

LESLIE H. GELB: I merely said it wasn't *inevitable* that we would intervene.

MARCUS G. RASKIN: That is fair enough. But you must be prepared to recognize other methods of intervention and engagement as part of the kit of American foreign policy.

III

DECISION-MAKING FOR ASIA:
OPTIONS OR COMPULSIONS?

Trade-offs
and Military Assistance

LEON SLOSS: The Nixon Doctrine is clearly a driving force now in shaping the military assistance program for Asia. The Doctrine has been somewhat maligned in this conference, but it is not too novel an experience to hear such criticism. Some of it is justified; some of it is not. There is a certain amount of ambiguity about this Doctrine. Some aspects of the Nixon Doctrine are being clarified. However, certain aspects are already clear and are expressed in the Doctrine itself. I don't need to elaborate on the three main points: (1) the U. S. intends to maintain its treaty commitments to our allies in Asia; (2) we will provide a shield for countries threatened by nuclear powers; and (3) we are looking primarily to other countries to defend themselves against indirect aggression and insurgency. One other thing is quite clear about the Nixon Doctrine: the U. S. is substantially reducing the number of its forces and bases in the Asian area. This is not only true of Vietnam and Korea, where such reductions have been much publicized; but it is also true of Thailand, the Philippines, Taiwan, and Japan. However, these reductions will not be precipitous. (Indeed, they are not rapid enough for many of the administration's critics.) But they will be scaled to the growing capacity of our allies to defend themselves.

On the other hand, there are a number of facets of the Nixon Doctrine which we within the government recognize as requiring further clarification. One of these is precisely how commitments are to be defined, particularly in this period of transition and change when we and some of our allies have different interpretations of these commitments. The formal treaty language frequently doesn't tell very much about what we should do in specific circumstances. And, indeed, I would argue that it is not desirable for us to be too precise about commitments. This attitude may offend some of the purists who would like to see more precision in our policy. I am not arguing for purposeful unclarity in policy, but making our commitments more precise runs into several pitfalls. There is likely to be a certain degradation of deterrence if we insist upon too much precision about what we would do in a specific circumstance. I would remind you of the familiar example of what happened in Korea when we tried to draw a hard and fast line. It is also clear that any effort to define commitments in a sense that would reassure our allies in Asia would present problems domestically; and conversely, any attempt to redefine or narrow commitments to be acceptable in the current political scene would not only create problems of confidence among our allies in Asia, but also could invite potential aggression in Asia. This is a dilemma—like so many we face in the real world of policy-making—that defies a precise solution.

One matter about which the Nixon Doctrine is not clear is what the U. S. will do in the event of a major non-nuclear overt aggression against an ally. This is the case that falls between the more clearly defined cases in the Nixon Doctrine. Here again, too clearly defined a policy may not be desirable.

Another major uncertainty, which has an important influence on the military assistance program, has to do with the respective roles of U. S. and allied forces in Asia. This is something which we are making an effort to clarify. Some things can be said about this. The Nixon Doctrine implies that the contribution of ground combat troops has to come largely, if not wholly, from local forces. But there could be some exceptions to this. The presence of some modest U. S. ground forces will continue to be important in the deterrent role in countries like Korea, and we are going to continue to have training establishments in a number of countries of Southeast Asia and East Asia. Current planning envisages maintenance of the Marine division on Okinawa. So while as a generalization the Nixon Doctrine implies no use of ground forces in Asia, there could be some exceptions to that generalization. We should, at least in my view, not be too dogmatic about it. For deterrent purposes, there are advantages in having a capability to introduce ground forces, even if our policy objective is to avoid that action.

As far as naval forces are concerned, the U. S. is the major naval power in the Pacific area and is likely to be so for a long time. It is unlikely that any of our allies will substitute in any major way for U. S. naval power, at least as far as a "blue ocean" navy is concerned. Having made this generalization, let me qualify it. There are some growing naval capabilities, particularly among the South Vietnamese forces, in coastal and inland waters. Also there is a question about the future naval role of Japan. Japan has argued that its forces are strictly for self-defense, and that is still its philosophy. But how Japan will interpret self-defense in the future is a question. Clearly Japan, by contrast with most other Asian nations, has the capacity to develop more than a token navy. Whether she will do so has yet to be seen.

The biggest question, however, has to do with air forces. Here is the area of U. S. military policy where our relationship to our allies is likely to be most severely tested. Even prior to the Nixon Doctrine, strictly in cost-effectiveness terms, it was held to be most efficient for the local nation to supply the ground forces and the U. S. to supply the air and naval forces. This would imply a limited role for the Asian countries in the air. The disadvantage of that, of course, is that it lowers the threshold of U. S. involvement in any conflict that might occur in Asia. If we are committed to provide all of the air support for local forces, our threshold of involvement may be very low, and the whole thrust of the Nixon Doctrine may be invalidated. On the other hand, a major role for our allies in the air is very costly, both for us in terms of equipment and for them in terms of maintenance. For many countries this conflicts with other objectives—notably that of economic and social development. It is just very hard to generalize about the relative roles of U. S. and allied air forces. It is going to differ from country to country.

Now let me say a few words about military assistance itself. First of all, I would like to stress some facts that are not always fully grasped. Military assistance takes a number of forms. It takes the form of grant assistance, credit sales under government auspices, commercial sales which may be facilitated by government-guaranteed financing, and the distribution of stocks which are excess to the needs of U. S. forces and which we offer at reduced rates. Attention has tended to focus on the grant program and to some extent on government-financed credit sales. Less attention has been given in the past to commercial sales and excess stocks. I would predict that these latter elements are going to be more important in terms of military transfers in the future.

There is another point that I would like to note. In the heyday of the Military Assistance Program, one year we asked Congress for $8 billion for military assistance. And we got something like $5 billion. We had a large program then for Europe, of course; but obviously, we are now talking about a very different situation. In fiscal year 1971 we have $350 million a year in grant assistance and have asked for, but have not obtained, some $750 million to finance credit sales. One of the implications of the Nixon Doctrine is a substantial increase in military assistance, specifically in Asia, at least for a period of time. It seems clear that the countries of this region of the world do not have the financial resources to create self-supporting military forces overnight. They must be at least partially supported by external resources if they are to become militarily self-sufficient. Furthermore, much of this must be grant aid or excess stocks until their capacity to repay loans increases. We will have a certain amount of excess stocks becoming available as we reduce our own force posture, but this is not as much of an asset as it may appear at first glance. A lot of this excess stock isn't the sort that the countries of Asia can use. Some of it is obsolete. For example, we are getting rid of a lot of naval vessels. Most of these are too old for effective operation or are not the kind of naval vessels that a country like Thailand, Vietnam, or even Korea could operate —destroyers, cruisers and aircraft carriers.

The general trend in Asia, however, is going to be a reduction of U. S. forces in the area and an increase in military assistance, and this is a good bargain—a favorable trade-off— for the United States. Take, for example, Korea. Here we propose to withdraw one division, the maintenance of which is costing us at least $400 million a year. If that division is demobilized, as we intend, the saving will be $2 billion over five years. Modernization of Korean forces may cost us $1 to $1½ billion over the same period. In strictly financial terms, this is a good bargain; but even more important, as U. S. forces are reduced and local capabilities are increased, the risk of our involvement in a minor conflict is minimized. Now, there are some practical political problems involved, and some real budgetary problems. We recognize that it isn't going to be easy to get increased funds for military assistance from the Congress. There is concern, largely on the basis of the Vietnam experience, that military assistance could be the first step to involvement in larger contingencies. In my own view, this is generalizing from the specific case of Vietnam. In fact it can be argued in the case of Korea, for example, that military assistance is the first step to withdrawal and not further involvement.

Let me say a word to bring this down to the kind of realities that we have to deal with on a day-to-day basis. In the first place, grant military assistance appropriations are at the lowest levels ever. The fiscal year 1970 credit sales program requested was around $750 million, and it never passed the Congress. Tacked onto it was the Cooper-Church Amendment, and consequently the appropriation bill was not passed. So the 1970 money to finance the sales program was not authorized by the Congress. That has had a substantial impact on our assistance programs, particularly for countries like Israel and Iran, although for Israel we finally did get authority to finance sales through the Jackson Amendment.

In the grant program, we have an annual authorization ceiling for the next two years of $350 million, which will not even maintain the forces we are now supporting. It provides no money for modernization. As the Secretary of Defense made clear in his posture statement in February 1970, this amount is, in the view of the Nixon administration, clearly inadequate. First there is Korea, where we have agreed to modernize Korean forces as our forces are withdrawn. I believe that the administration's request for a supplemental appropriation for Korea has a good chance of acceptance by the Congress because, as I have previously noted, it reflects sound policy and sound economics and is fully consistent with the Nixon Doctrine. Indeed it is the first major test case of the Congress's willingness to accept that doctrine. Then we have the Cambodia request for which there might be more skepticism in Congress. Nevertheless, we have the problem of how to disengage from our involvement in Cambodia without leaving complete chaos. This certainly will involve some military assistance over and above anything we planned for at the beginning of 1970. If that weren't enough, then came the Middle East situation with immense requirements, if we are going to maintain our commitment to Israel and maintain a balance of power in the area. This is on the sales side of the program, but it is a very large amount, nevertheless. And we have had the crisis in Jordan.[1] Who knows what requirements may yet

1. In January 1971, Congress passed supplementary legislation providing for grant military assistance of $150 million for Korea, $185 million for

arise in the Middle East? Inevitably, when you have to deal with contingencies, the unexpected is the rule rather than the exception.

Now, in the era when we had several billion dollars for military assistance, it was relatively easy to accommodate this sort of contingency. But when we have $350 million of grant assistance and no credit sales program authorized, it presents a real problem. What we had to do temporarily was to divert substantial funds from very important but lower priority programs, such as Turkey and Taiwan. Funds for these programs already were the minimum required to maintain existing forces and the programs should be brought back up to the minimum.

I have presented a concept of how we might proceed in our military assistance program to be consistent with the Nixon Doctrine. But it is going to be hard even to get on to this long term basis until we can see our way through the immediate crises.

EARL C. RAVENAL: Some might argue that the very fact that unexpected contingencies always arise in some part of the world—each having its own requirements for emergency assistance—is just another illustration of the open-ended and uncontrollable nature of our whole stance of intervention. This stance has not changed a bit, but rather is exemplified by the Nixon Doctrine. I say that with all due respect to your day-to-day labors in coping with these crises. But given a continuation of our interest in all the places in the world where such things arise, one could predict that your burdens are never going to be lightened, and the pressures on the government to divert military assistance will never be eased.

MARCUS G. RASKIN: The United States has commitments in various parts of the world. The Nixon Doctrine

Cambodia, and $30 million for Jordan; and military credits of $500 million for Israel.

states that the United States will live up to its commitments. What does it get in return for these commitments?

LEON SLOSS: That is a matter of opinion. Let me give you my own personal philosophy on this. It may sound old-fashioned, but I feel it is valid. We live in a relatively small world. Events that occur in distant places do affect our own society directly. The U. S. has a stake in law and order in this world—as in our own local communities where we have a stake in law and order in the community. There are parts of the world were we have important interests, and those interests are threatened when there isn't order and stability. There is going to be instability in many of these countries, but if violence and aggression can take place and there are no inhibitions, the they are going to spread. U. S. investments and commercial interests will be at stake, the lives of U. S. citizens can be jeopardized if there is violence, and in the long run the very quality of our own lives will be affected by the kind of societies we coexist with on this planet.

MARCUS G. RASKIN: Are you saying that what the United States gets is a commitment on the part of the host government to keep law and order in that particular part of the world?

LEON SLOSS: Well, we can't, of course, impose law and order on other countries, but it is obviously in our interest that they maintain order and that we don't have to intervene to protect U. S. interests. All of us would agree that it would be a terrible tragedy if we have to put American troops in a country to save American citizens or property. The fact that a country can maintain law and order by itself reduces this risk.

FRANZ SCHURMANN: I get the sense that military assistance will be a substitute for ground forces or for certain other kinds of military input. To the extent that the United States withdraws from Asia and withdrawal is compensated by increased military assistance, isn't that going to create a balance of payments problem? A lot of people in the financial and business world say this is adversely affecting the economy. Aren't we just substituting one drain of dollars abroad for another drain?

LEON SLOSS: In the first place, the balance of payments problem is not the whole story. One has to weigh the advantages of alleviating the payments deficit against the advantages we are getting from the program. I think the balance of payments deficit we have incurred is justified by the gain. On the whole, it is more than worth it. In the long run the drain on our balance of payments is going to be less. For example, we spent something like $450 million in 1970 to maintain one of the two divisions in Korea. Only a part of that was a drain on the balance of payments, as much of it consisted of manpower costs and equipment purchased in the U. S. The program we are proposing for Korea provides $1 to $1½ billion over a five-year period in military assistance, most of which will be goods and services purchased in the United States. So that is not going to be a substantial drain on the balance of payments. Over the long run I would hope that we could transfer this program to a credit sales basis, for which we would be eventually reimbursed; but that is going to involve extending some long-term credits to a country like Korea. Hopefully, five years from now, they will have the capacity to pay for it. But we would be exacerbating the problem now by moving to credit sales too rapidly.

Local forces cannot substitute for U. S. forces in all cases. For the foreseeable future we must have some U. S. ground forces in Korea as an element of insurance. Their very presence will serve as a deterrent to Chinese aggression. It does not have to be a large force to accomplish this purpose. Also, in the next decade not very many Asian countries will be able to pursue the air and naval role that the U. S. is now assuming. So we are not talking about a total withdrawal of American power. We are talking about a very substantial reduction, and some efforts are necessary to build up local forces to compensate for that.

MARCUS G. RASKIN: You used the instance of Korea, where military assistance might allow us to pull out. Aren't there many more cases where military assistance is likely to cause further escalation? Aren't you concerned by the reinforcement that military assistance gives to instability?

LEON SLOSS: Yes, I am concerned. But I don't take the view that arms themselves will create wars. Opportunities create wars. While we would certainly like to see lower levels of armaments, for example in the Middle East, we haven't found any formula for doing this so long as the Soviet Union continues to pour in massive amounts of military assistance. If we do nothing to offset that, then there would be an imbalance, which would invite war. I wish there were a better solution to that problem, but I don't see any simple one. We are trying to exercise restraint in arms sales while maintaining a reasonable balance.

RICHARD F. KAUFMAN: Aren't you really saying that under the Nixon Doctrine, the substitution of military assistance and weapons for ground forces will permit the United States to continue its policy of intervention at bargain rates, to the extent that military assistance is cheaper than the current level of ground forces?

LEON SLOSS: I wouldn't quite put it that way. There is a difference between providing arms so that others can maintain their own security and providing U. S. forces. At least we have some options when U. S. ground forces are not on the line and when U. S. air and naval forces are standing offshore. If we have 65,000 men near the Korean demilitarized zone and the North Koreans attack, we don't have an option.

RICHARD F. KAUFMAN: Well, if there were only five or ten thousand, instead of 65,000, would we have more of an option, if North Korea attacked South Korea?

LEON SLOSS: In my view we would definitely have more of an option.

RICHARD F. KAUFMAN: Even though the 10,000 were more endangered by virtue of their small numbers than the 65,000 would be?

LEON SLOSS: It is only an assumption that they would be endangered. Eventually, I would hope that the 10,000, or whatever the number is, would be behind the lines in support functions. It is our objective and our belief that South Korean ground forces can cope with North Korean ground forces. U. S. combat involvement on the ground wouldn't be required at all.

EARL C. RAVENAL: There is a paradox here. If it is cheap and cost-advantageous to withdraw U. S. forces, this logic should prevail down to the last U. S. soldier. It should be cost-effective to bring U. S. forces down to zero. Now, what continuing function does the presence of a small and practically useless American force serve except to give evidence of a commitment; that is, to commit us and deny us the option which you say the Nixon Doctrine is attempting to create?

LEON SLOSS: In the purest sense, their function is to deter the Chinese and the North Koreans. It is true that if we had no forces, there would be less involvement, and there may come a time when we will have no military forces in Korea. But if we have 10,000 men behind the demilitarized zone, our involvement in a North Korean attack would be less than if we had 65,000 on the front lines. It is not going to eliminate the risk of involvement. But it is going to reduce it, and it will give us more options. And it is by no means clear that complete withdrawal reduces the risk of involvement. Witness Korea in 1950.

RICHARD A. FALK: Are you advancing a view of a special American mission in the world, or is this a mission that you would accord to every major government?

LEON SLOSS: Obviously, the United States is not every major government. We have more interests than many, simply because we are what we are. That does not mean, however, that our interests are universal or that they are undifferentiated. But the United States, as a major power, does have interests that Luxembourg doesn't have, or even the United Kingdom or Japan. That is just a fact of life.

RICHARD A. FALK: If other leading governments were to follow the lines of policy-making that you are advocating for the United States, it would tend to yield very inflammatory confrontations whenever perceived interests converged on a struggle going on in a foreign society. The logic of such a position is to induce an escalatory spiral of interventionary and counterinterventionary moves.

LEON SLOSS: As a matter of fact, recent history shows us that where the interests of major powers overlap, there may be a basis for a stalemate and a good bit of caution. Particularly where there is clearly a dominant interest of one major power and a lesser interest of another major power, there is a reasonably stable situation, at least as far as great power conflict is concerned. Examples are Eastern Europe on the one hand and Latin America on the other. It is where interests are fairly evenly balanced, as in the Middle East, that the risk of a confrontation is increased.

WILLIAM W. WHITSON: I would like to raise a question on the operational side of the Nixon Doctrine. That is the problem of calculating the gap in capabilities for a client country. Who would make this estimate? In the past, our military advisory groups calculated it. How would that process be carried forward under the new arrangement so as to arrive at a realistic notion of shortfall?

LEON SLOSS: There is no science to this. You do the best you can with the resources available. A lot of political judgment goes into this. It is useful to have the estimates of the military advisory teams as to what the requirements are. Their estimates are almost always far in excess of what we can afford to do. So there must be a judgment process. We are always going to be working with far less money than military experts tell us we need to do the military job.

DANIEL ELLSBERG: I don't think you addressed a critical question: under the Nixon Doctrine, to what extent must U. S. air power and nuclear weapons be more implicit right behind the first line of defense in the effort of Asian containment?

LEON SLOSS: That is a matter that is still very much debated in the government, especially the nuclear question. We may end up two years from now with a good deal less capacity in Asia than we have had in the past. But there is still a very substantial capacity left. U. S. air power for a long time will have to stand behind the local ground forces.

But the question of nuclear weapons touches on a rather sensitive issue. I will not go into the details of that. There is one point of view that says that if we have the same commitments and we must reduce forces, the only thing we can do is substitute nuclear weapons to fill the gap. My own view is that this is a very ill thought-through proposition which doesn't stand up after you peel the first layer off. It is very difficult to substitute nuclear weapons for ground forces or air forces in an intervention role. There are too many inhibitions on our use of nuclear weapons. I think we should have them in the theater, and I think they would always remain an ultimate deterrent. But I think that the practical circumstances under which we could use them are extremely limited.

MILTON KOTLER: Do you approach military assistance with a view to equipping a government with the full capability to defend itself, or do you equip it only with what is necessary in view of the presence of our own weapons? If we do the latter it makes it necessary for us always to make the political judgment and commitment to use the "other half" of the equipment—that is, our own.

LEON SLOSS: That is a problem, particularly in the case of air power. This really varies, depending upon what country and what scenario we are looking at. We are equipping each country to have a self-defense capability under certain circumstances and short of other circumstances. For example, it is clear to us that the South Koreans, with the forces that they now have and a certain amount of mobilization, can cope with a North Korean attack without any U. S. help on the ground, but with some U. S. help in the air. On the other hand, the North Korean air force is a larger and more modern force than the South Korean air force. Now, you may say that will inevitably involve us. That may be true. But an effort to make the Korean air force self-sufficient, at least in the short run, would be terribly costly, both for us and for them.

Defense Planning
and Military Capabilities

PIERRE M. SPREY: There is a very common tendency to overestimate the extent of rationality in defense planning, whether in U. S. force structure or military assistance. This is a great mistake and leads to a serious misunderstanding of the Department of Defense as an institution. The content of rationality and systematic planning in defense force structures and budgets is actually relatively low. There are some who say that this is inevitably so, that defense cannot be managed under any scheme. Since I disagree with this view, I am going to give a tourist's guide to the types of schemes for managing defense. I will end with some comments on the Nixon-Laird management of defense and where it stands among the various feasible schemes.

There are two basic poles in managing defense. One is the "buy what we need" approach, which was what McNamara brought in. Interestingly enough, Henry Kissinger was one of the forerunners in introducing that approach in some of his publications from 1955 to 1960. Nevertheless, when McNamara first confronted Congress with the statement that he had analyzed our defense needs and determined what they were, Congress was totally astonished. There was a famous exchange in which Chairman Rivers asked McNamara in a tone of complete incredulity whether he actually intended to determine the exact defense needs of the nation. McNamara answered with a flat yes. The other pole in defense management is the fixed budget or fixed cost approach: this entails doing the best we can within a fixed budget level that is set by a number of factors, including political and economic considerations.

Take the first approach, "buy what we need." The most important element of any management scheme in the Department of Defense is clearly the motivational element: that is, the type of motivations that the scheme induces in the Defense Department's constituent departments, that is, the Services. The motivational element is the Achilles' heel of the "buy what we need" approach. Unfortunately, it appears to be bureaucratically inevitable that if you start with the idea that we should determine and then buy what we need, you will very rapidly be forced into the posture of defending a fixed force structure. This is exactly what happened to McNamara. In his first year, with the help of the early "whiz kids," he came up with a quick analysis of what he thought he needed. Then he spent seven years defending the conclusions of that first quick analysis. In other words, he became locked into a fixed force structure, and he continued to manage the Department of Defense not by fixed dollar levels but by fixed numbers of force units. By that I mean numbers of carriers, divisions, and squadrons of airplanes.

This in turn had a serious motivational effect on Defense's constituents. This effect can be seen very simply. You are sitting in the position of a chief of staff and the boss has said that you will have X carriers and no more. Furthermore, it appears that policy is going to last for quite a while. The first thing you do, of course, is emphasize that the level is inadequate. To do that, you come in with beefed-up estimates of what enemy forces can do and emphasize how inadequate our forces are in the face of the large and increasing threat. Naturally, since you are not being managed by fixed dollar levels, you underestimate the costs of proposed programs. It is this motivational factor that underlies the large number of major cost overruns we have had in the last ten years.

Finally—and this is, from the point of view of actual expenditures, among the more serious problems—you take each one of these forces, the fifteen carriers, nineteen divisions, or whatever they are, and you make this force unit as multimission, as expensive, as "capable," and as gold-plated as possible. You have little choice in this area, since it is the only means you have left to expand your Service.

Defense has inherited a plethora of extremely expensive acquisition programs that started under McNamara. They were started with the express purpose of increasing the "capability" of a fixed number of force units. This is perhaps the fundamental reason we have had a cost explosion in defense hardware. The cost of individual units of defense hardware has increased far faster than the national price level. The rate of increase in the price of tanks, destroyers, airplanes, etc., since World War II has outstripped inflation in the general economy by factors of 5 to 100, depending on the hardware involved.

The other approach—"fixed cost"—has its own set of problems and deficiencies, though in somewhat different areas. The most fundamental problem is that, in the face of fixed cost, the Services will try to eliminate mundane though essential items while preserving those hardware systems and units that are most glamorous and most prestigious from the point of view of senior officers. The result is serious inadequacy in common and uninteresting inventories: beans and bullets and training and logistics. As is well known, the shocking unreadiness of the armed forces in 1960 was due almost entirely to the uncontrolled tendency of the Services to cut support under the 1954–1960 "fixed cost" policy. So either way, whether you advocate the fixed force structure approach or the fixed cost approach, the advantages to the Department of Defense are by no means automatic. My own preference is for the fixed cost approach, since I believe it is considerably easier to control underspending in beans and bullets than it is to control the limitless gold plating of every conceivable weapons system.

In practice, a significant reason why the "buy what we need" approach worked so badly is ultimately based on the limitations of analysis of force requirements. The naive analyst's view is that if we only had a firm national strategy, we could determine the forces needed to implement that strategy and thus settle defense problems rationally. This is a major illusion. In fact, the state of analysis of overall force requirements—strategic forces as well as conventional ground, naval, and air forces—is very primitive, far more primitive than public propaganda would indicate. The only analytical tools available for such force analyses are a class of models that I would characterize as nothing more than attrition models. These originated as a set of elementary differential equations that simply describe losses on both sides. They were formulated around World War I by a mathematician named Lanchester. Since then, a great many variations have been played on the same theme. Many complexities have been introduced in an attempt to improve the realism of these models. Unfortunately, both the old and the new models are nothing more than reasonable-sounding hypotheses; they were and remain scientifically unvalidated by empirical or historical data.

Interestingly enough, these tools appear always to lead to the same type of predictions—predictions that have a major impact on policy decisions, as I will demonstrate. First, let me explain what these predictions look like. Let us assume you are predicting outcomes against a fixed threat. On one axis—the X axis—you have the forces you need in order to meet that threat, stated in terms of the ratio to the threat force level. On the other axis—the Y axis—you have the probability of winning with that ratio of forces. (This is quite independent of whether you are talking about ground forces or airplanes. The trend predicted by any of the attrition models always has the same behavior.) Starting at the left of the curve with very inferior forces, say a one-to-five inferiority to the threat, you achieve a very low probability of victory. As you move to the right towards one-to-one forces, your chances of victory improve very steeply. By the time you are up to a two-to-one ratio, you have a very high probability of winning. By the time you are up to five-to-one, you have a virtual certainty of winning.

It is interesting to plot the same thing for actual historical engagements. You get a very interesting curve—a very *different* curve—and there is a serious policy implication here. The historical curve has a very slow increase in probability of victory as forces increase. The implication is highly significant: one must conclude that it is impossible to predict even approximately the outcome of battles and wars on the basis of force quantities alone. The outcome will be uncertain even when you have great force superiority. For example, with a crushing force advantage of five-to-one, you may have only an 80 percent chance of winning. So it is by no means clear that simply because you have a huge army or large quantities of military hardware that you are going to carry the day. This is a point that is simply not presented to policy-makers; most particularly it has never been presented by the Joint Chiefs of Staff, or even by the Secretary of Defense.

Now, I don't mean to imply that the Joint Chiefs of Staff actually believe in these models or theoretical attrition equations. They are simply useful tools for advocacy. When the tools are questioned, the military fall back on much more classical rules of thumb—the old rules from the Infantry School: for example, it takes a two-to-one force ratio to attack successfully; you can stand up to one-and-a-half-to-one inferiority when defending; and other such rules. But even these rules have the same defects as the Lanchesterian type of analysis: they sound firmer than they are. Unfortunately, despite the fact that current analysis of large-scale force engagements totally lacks scientific credibility, it is used to create a dangerously false impression of predictability and precision at the highest policy-making levels.

I have at least briefly reviewed for you the chief defects of the "buy what we need" approach: namely, the impossibility of even approximately determining the quantities needed, and the perverse incentives created by the associated fixed force structure goals. Changing from the critical to the constructive, I would like to point out some of the interesting possibilities under a seriously managed fixed cost approach. The most interesting of those possibilities is shown, for example, in an analysis of two alternative equal cost tactical air forces: one represents our current approach with highly complex gold-plated aircraft, while the other is an approach based only on aircraft carefully tailored for both maximum austerity *and* higher performance. It can be seen that there is a tremendous swing in the size of the forces you can have within a fixed dollar level (or taking it the other way, if you want to hold a force constant, you can change costs very radically without changing capabilities). The analysis shows that our current approach yields a force of 1,200 first-line tactical airplanes that cost $32 billion over ten years, a number roughly representative of current plans. But you could substitute the austere force (consisting of individual single-purpose aircraft types, in each case more effective than the ones they displace in the current approach) and wind up with the same cost and a force of 4,200 considerably superior airplanes.

Now, exactly the same procedure can be used for every force in our inventory and similar results can be achieved. The same magnitude of change can be achieved in strategic forces, land forces, and sea forces. This is the essential attraction of managing by fixed costs: it introduces the possibility of effecting not just small efficiencies and small changes in defense expenditures, but changes by factors of three and greater.

The preceding discussion has really been a relatively theoretical model of two different ways of managing the Department of Defense. Looking at the day-to-day actualities of Defense, the Nixon-Laird management has developed quite a bit of rhetoric over the last two years on how it has kept the best elements of the McNamara management of defense but has merely determined the "right" budget at the White House level, and below that has implemented that "right" budget through fiscal guidance. To implement this, there is a whole new vocabulary and alphabet soup of memorandums and programs and planning documents. But in fact, that system and that vocabulary represent only the appearances of planning. The rhetoric covers the fact that the Nixon-Laird management is not oriented to close management control of the Department of Defense at all.

With very rare exceptions, the real operating policy for Defense is simply to lay out a budget level that it can live with; then to let the constituent military departments take their piece of that pie and do with it pretty much as they please. Now, this is exactly the way that Charles Wilson managed the Defense Department. The rhetoric, of course, serves its purpose, because managing the Department of Defense the way Charles Wilson did is not really acceptable today, not even to Congress.

From the point of view of policy-making, the key implication of the Nixon-Laird management approach is that in fact the so-called national strategy decisions have negligible effect on what actually goes on in Defense. That is, we could institute a 1½ war policy or a 7 war policy; we could institute 30-day logistics guidance for wars in Europe or 360-day logistics guidance for wars in Europe; we could continue to have men in Asia or completely restructure our strategy so as not to fight on the Asian mainland—no fundamental programs would change in the Department of Defense, since it is not being effectively controlled. The Department of Defense continues to buy those forces and programs that senior officers find attractive for one reason or another, and the only thing that changes is the rhetoric under which they are bought. A classic example of this phenomenon is the F-111. The F-111 was originally conceived and justified (circa 1958) to become the nuclear arm of the Tactical Air Command so that it could compete with the Strategic Air Command. McNamara changed the rhetoric. He justified the F-111 (starting in 1962) as a multi-purpose airplane designed for conventional operations. We are still buying F-111's, and the rhetoric is that the aircraft will support the Nixon Doctrine and help us to disengage. All these changes in justification have been expended on an airplane whose fundamental design and capabilities have not changed one iota from 1959 until today. The F-111 example is a microcosm of the influence of national strategy and policy on the day-to-day operations of the Department of Defense.

What are the key points for people who are interested in policy? Stated negatively, my best advice is at least to avoid the following three illusions: The first illusion is that national policy decisions influence anything but defense rhetoric. The second illusion is that if, miraculously, we were given a clear-cut national strategy that formed a cohesive and consistent and predictable policy, it would be possible to estimate from the ground up the defense requirements to implement it. That is simply not possible. Real defense decisions (as opposed to analytical exercises) have always been based on small incremental changes from existing force and budget levels—these decisions almost never encompass overall defense budget changes of more than plus or minus 10 percent. The third illusion—very prevalent in the early McNamara days—is that you can buy defense forces by the yard: if you spend twice as much, you can buy twice as much "capability," twice as much performance, or cover twice as many commitments. In fact the amount of expenditure has very little relationship to the amount of "capability." On the contrary, we have seen that it is possible to change the size and effectiveness of forces by at least a factor of three without any change in expense.

LEON SLOSS: I would like to challenge the preceding characterization of the Nixon-Laird defense budgeting system.

Although I sit in the State Department, I have dealt with the defense budget for twenty years, and I am still involved as more than an observer of this process. Of course there is a gap between rhetoric and reality. There always has been. But in attempting to understand and deal with security policy we can't rely on a caricature of reality.

That is what we were presented: a very gross caricature of how this system really works. It is true that no secretary of defense has ever had complete management grasp of the defense budget. It is just too big and too complicated. But it is obvious that over the past ten years there has been a remarkable increase in the capability of the secretary of defense to manage the Department of Defense.

It is still far from perfect. No system has been perfect. It was far from perfect with McNamara, and there was a lot of rhetoric which tended to exaggerate the degree of control. But only if you are postulating an ideal world in which every single procurement decision is related back to some ideal strategy—only then does the system fall short of adequacy. It is very unrealistic to suggest that there is no control or no relationship between procurement decisions, strategy, and policy. The system does tend to do this. Even though it is done imperfectly, it is being done a lot better today than ten or fifteen years ago. So I wouldn't want the impression to be left that the system is totally ineffective.

RICHARD F. KAUFMAN: It is appropriate for me to take strong issue with Leon Sloss and to reinforce what Pierre Sprey said about the unmanageability of the Defense Department. Mr. Sloss would be in a very small minority today, even in defense management circles, if he were to maintain that the management of procurement is more automatically related to strategy and more efficient than it was a decade ago, or a few years ago, or in any historical period. That is illustrated by recent events and confessions by politicians and high officials of the Defense Department, including Mr. Packard, who said to a convention of defense managers in California that procurement is a mess. The Fitzhugh Commission said as much.

LESLIE H. GELB: It is deplorable how readily we turn off our ears to each other and put words in the mouths of each other. Mr. Kaufman has accused Mr. Sloss of saying that procurement in the Defense Department was automatically related to strategy. Mr. Sloss did not say that. He said only that procurement decisions are not wholly unrelated to strategy.

RICHARD F. KAUFMAN: The issue is whether or not there has been a general decline in management capability within the Defense Department, particularly in the area of procurement—whether that would be an accurate description or a "caricature." Leon Sloss said it was a caricature; that in fact our management capabilities were improving over time; that McNamara had contributed to the improvement; and that current policies were continuing the trend of improvement in capability. My point was that management, at least insofar as it is reflected in procurement, is certainly not improving, by all the evidence.

MARCUS G. RASKIN: Let's assume for a moment that strategy and procurement *are* related. Let's assume that the system worked perfectly. Now, how does that relate to the issue that Richard Falk has presented: that is, a very different perception of what the world is about? Whether or not procurement and strategic analysis are related is not really the point. The point is that there are very different views of the world that are held very strongly. The technocratic notion is that you can back out of the underlying question, which is the view of the world that you hold. I think we shouldn't back out of that question.

Concepts
and Force Structures

LEONARD RODBERG: I would like to make three comments on the way force planning and the force structure will probably go. The first is that, because of economic and political considerations, the defense budget probably will stay about where it is for the next few years. It certainly will not be able to go up very much. I don't know what success the Congress will have in cutting the defense budget back, but it will not go up very much. Given inflation, the Defense Department is going to have to cut some place, and force levels are most likely to be cut back, particularly the level of men maintained in the United States. One of the things the Defense Department has learned from Vietnam is that the active reserve forces maintained in the continental United States are not useful even in a "half war" such as Vietnam. When we really became involved, the level of American manpower directly involved on the land was such that we had to increase substantially the number of men we had in the armed forces. The increased conventional capabilities that had been built up during the four or five years of McNamara really didn't count for very much when they actually got involved. Also, the Pentagon seems to have concluded that the so-called nonnuclear option is unreal. If we don't have enough manpower to win a Vietnam war, we clearly don't have enough to fight a Chinese war. The nonnuclear option *never* had any reality, and today people are explicitly recognizing that. You hear them now talking about the use of reserves in the kind of situation where they might want to involve American troops. In other words, they are planning to have conventional forces available, in spite of the Nixon Doctrine, but not necessarily in an active status—which means active forces can be cut back and the savings put into other things.

The second comment is that, in spite of the so-called Nixon Doctrine, there is still no intention ever to lose any piece of territory that we have chosen to consider within the perimeter of our commitments. Rather than lose, we will introduce American forces. A recent example of this was Jordan: if 400 Americans had not been living there, they would have had to be invented as an excuse for the introduction of American troops. Reductions might come in force levels, but our other capabilities for intervention have not been reduced. We are keeping an extensive air and sea lift force, including C-5As and C-141s, new LHA assault ships and new commercial ships that are being built for charter to the navy, to maintain military forces and military supplies in convenient places overseas. The base network is also being maintained. Some bases, of course, are being closed down. But the network is intact. And many of the troops coming out of Vietnam, of course, are going elsewhere overseas.

The Laird defense budget is still a McNamara style budget—that is, a budget which has the capacity in dollars continuously to modernize the forces for intervention: tactical air, helicopter units, and new technology. The fact that they are being modernized means that we either intend to use them ourselves or sell them to other people. It means that there are going to be American advisors, and that means American engagement in every country in which our technology is made available. Military aid, whether it comes through AID (Agency for International Development) or through other forms of making our technology available, inevitably involves the presence of Americans.

We may not be reverting to "fortress America," but rather to "capital-base America," where the technology we have for intervention is available either in this country or at overseas bases, initially involving small numbers of Americans, but eventually larger numbers if they become necessary.

All of this involves a third point: that is, bureaucracy. The Defense Department structure is being maintained intact, and the ideology that goes with it is still believed. The structure is predicated on an intervention policy which hasn't changed. To put it crudely, there has been no real change in the structure of the American defense establishment for at least a twenty-year period.

Options and
Tactical Nuclear Weapons

STANLEY M. KANAROWSKI: The comments that follow describe how one might go about analyzing the role of
nuclear weapons under the Nixon Doctrine. Anything like a
full treatment of this subject would be well beyond the scope
of this conference; accordingly, and necessarily, what follows
will be schematic in nature. Moreover, I would like to say
these comments are my views and do not reflect the position
of the Nixon administration or the various government agencies with which I have been associated.

By way of background, the U. S. has maintained nuclear-
capable forces in the Pacific since the early 1950s. During the
1950s, when the U. S. had an effective monopoly of nuclear
forces, our policy was basically a "massive retaliation" nuclear
policy. Gradually, with the changing U. S.-Soviet nuclear balance, and with questions about the credibility of massive retaliation, this policy shifted toward "flexible response," with an
increased emphasis on conventional capabilities.

In Guam on July 25, 1969, and in his November 3, 1969,
address, President Nixon said:

> The United States will keep all its treaty commitments. We
> shall provide a shield if a nuclear power threatens the free-
> dom of a nation allied with us, or of a nation whose survival
> we consider vital to our security and the security of the re-

gion as a whole. In cases involving other types of aggressions, we shall furnish military and economic assistance when requested in accordance with our treaty commitments. But we shall look to the nation directly threatened to assume the primary responsibility of providing the manpower for its defense.

One might say, as earlier discussions have, that this is as specific as a president can be about his doctrine. What I would like to suggest, in the comments to follow, is the context in which this policy might be analyzed. This context involves: (1) our nuclear assurances, (2) nuclear proliferation, (3) relationships between our Asian and our Soviet policies, (4) the nature of the military threat, and (5) the conventional posture of our allies and our own forces.

The first consideration is our nuclear assurances, which are covered in a variety of documents. The most general assurances are set forth in the U. N. Charter. More specific assurances are to be found in our formal bilateral and multilateral treaties with our allies in Asia and the Pacific. The most specific commitments have been made by the president in various statements. The U. N. Charter obligates the U. S. in the broadest sense to contribute to the maintenance of international peace and security. U. N. Security Council Resolution 255 (1968) binds the U. S., as well as others, to recognize that nuclear aggression or threats of aggression against a nonnuclear state would require the nuclear-capable permanent members of the Security Council to act immediately, through the Security Council, and to take the measures necessary to counter the aggression in accordance with the U. N. Charter. The U. S. is also a party to four bilateral treaties in Asia (Japan, Korea, Taiwan, Philippines) and two multilateral treaties: ANZUS (Australia, New Zealand) and SEATO (South Vietnam, Thailand, Philippines, Pakistan, the United Kingdom, and France). These agreements are all vague with respect to the nature of the U. S. response to any aggression. They all commit the signatories, in the event of an armed attack on any of the parties, to meet the common danger in accordance with constitutional processes.

Presidential statements have amplified these commitments. For example, in October 1964, following the first nuclear explosion in China, President Johnson said: "The nations that do not seek national nuclear weapons can be sure that, if they need our strong support against some threat of nuclear blackmail, then they will have it." And as mentioned above, President Nixon at Guam stated: "We will provide a shield if a nuclear power threatens an ally or a nation whose survival we consider vital to our security." Various speakers today have commented on the applicability of these commitments in the context of the Nixon Doctrine. One might summarize two views: One holds that our commitments are described in very general terms and do not require a specific force response; therefore, we need not consider modifying these commitments in accordance with changes in our military strategy or capabilities. Against this view, others point out that the Nixon Doctrine will reduce our ability to meet commitments; therefore, we should consider modifying past assurances and commitments accordingly.

The second factor is the proliferation of nuclear weapons in Asia. The Soviets and Chinese already have a nuclear capability. Beyond this, three Asian countries—India, Japan, and Australia—are said to have the technical know-how for initiating a nuclear weapons program. Other Asian countries, such as Taiwan, Korea, and Thailand, probably have very little capability in this respect and do not appear to be making any effort to change this situation. A number of factors—including the Non-Proliferation Treaty, U. S. relations with the Chinese and Soviets, and the direction of long-term Japanese policy —will probably affect proliferation in the future. Japan, Taiwan, and Australia have signed the Non-Proliferation Treaty. For these countries the Non-Proliferation Treaty would become a constraint on development of nuclear weapons, since they would be obliged to give other parties and the U. N. Security Council a formal three month advance notice and an explanation of the extraordinary events which caused the decision to withdraw. In addition, safeguards on spread of materials and technology would also become an obstacle to proliferation, especially for countries which need nuclear-related imports for a weapons program. The significance of this obstacle would be increased when the treaty is widely followed, according to Articles III and X.

From a strategic viewpoint, the Japanese intention with respect to development of nuclear weapons is probably the central proliferation issue. The Japanese have signed the Non-Proliferation Treaty. Whether or not they will ratify it, however, is an open question. By not ratifying the treaty, some say that Japan has preserved an option in the nuclear area. They argue that this course may make China, the USSR, and the U. S. hesitate in adopting policies which might become a cause for the Japanese to produce their own nuclear weapons. On the other hand, the Japanese are not likely to consider officially any proposals for a nuclear weapons program. There is no apparent support for nuclear weapons in the power centers: the political parties, press, business community and powerful parts of the bureaucracy (that is, the Ministries of Finance and International Trade and Industry). Even though Prime Minister Sato has said that defensive nuclear weapons would not be unconstitutional (Prime Minister Kishi took substantially the same position ten years ago), he has also reaffirmed Japan's three nuclear principles (no manufacture, possession, or importation of nuclear weapons).

A third consideration is the SALT discussions (the Strategic Arms Limitation Talks). Some commentators have pointed out that there is a direct relationship between the nuclear shield in Asia and an antiballistic missile system. They argue that a thin ABM defense is needed in order to make the Nixon Doctrine more credible. On the other hand, they point out that our rationale for an ABM system could become, in the eyes of the Chinese, an aggressive policy. This particular line of reasoning has been expounded by Doak Barnett in his April 1970 *Foreign Affairs* article.

The fourth consideration is the nature of the threat in Asia, as perceived by our allies and in terms of our own interests. Analysts, over the years, have come to discuss three major Asian theaters—Southeast Asia, Taiwan, and Korea. There has been a tendency to concentrate on the fact that China, North Vietnam, and North Korea all keep large armies which could be employed in overt operations if China felt its interests were challenged. Many analysts also appear to believe that the Chinese prefer and have found a low-cost way of expanding their own power—through economic expansion and insurgency operations. By building roads into more remote provinces, into Tibet and into northern and southern Laos, they have succeeded in changing the direction of trade patterns. Commerce and contacts which had normally flowed down into the southern countries now are going into China, and accordingly the Chinese have gained influence over the mountain people. Eventually, this line of reasoning goes, they would hope to expand further into Southeast Asia.

A fifth consideration is our conventional posture. Many believe that if we reduce our conventional capabilities in Asia, we must refine our commitments or build up our allies; otherwise nuclear war could become our only military option.

What are the consequences of this latter military option—actually using nuclear weapons? To answer this question a number of factors bear consideration: (1) the specific strategic and tactical gains we might anticipate from using nuclear weapons; (2) the range of responses that might be expected from the force we were opposing; and (3) the range of worldwide reactions and consequences. The decision-maker must interrelate these considerations, balancing risks and gains.

With respect to the first factor, the gains from the using of weapons, analysts traditionally have focused either on strategic or tactical issues. On the strategic side, some argue that tactical nuclear weapons may open up new options. They might open up a preemption option, for example, similar to the Israelis' attack on the Egyptian air force in 1967. Speaking hypothetically, if a fleet were massing for an assault on Taiwan, or if large Chinese forces were massing in North Korea or Southeast Asia, or if a large air deployment had taken place, pre-emption would be a strategic option. There was a long article discussing this possibility in the *National Observer* in 1969, by William Van Cleve, now a senior official in the Department of Defense. He indicated, at the extreme, that in a crisis it would be useful to be able to disarm the Chinese nuclear capability or selectively disarm the airpower capabilities of the North Koreans or North Vietnamese.

Aside from strategic options, there are tactical options which might provide gains in efficiency. For example, since interdiction costs so much in conventional firepower, one might look to tactical nuclear weapons to do that job more efficiently. The nuclear weapons designed for fighting in Europe during the late 1950s include, for example, artillery, mines, and surface-to-surface rockets. Each of these systems provide a large increase in lethality over conventional weapons systems. Accordingly, one can make an argument that using these weapons allows a smaller number of divisions and aircraft to do a much bigger job much faster. (A related line of reasoning was used by General MacArthur when he analyzed the cost of an invasion of Japan in 1945. He estimated that roughly 500,000 casualties over a year would be incurred in an invasion of Japan. His analysis became a factor—though not necessarily the critical one—in the decision to bomb Hiroshima and Nagasaki.)

As indicated at the outset, it is unreal to talk about technical military gains without looking at a second factor—the possible costs. First, strictly from the military point of view, the Chinese could counterattack with nuclear weapons. They could respond by hitting a logistic base, such as Inchon or Pusan in Korea, with a view to stopping the flow of critical items for allied or our own ground forces. Alternatively, the

Chinese might respond without nuclear escalation, but simply by continuing to fight conventionally. One might hypothesize that their army is large, that they could draw back, regroup, and after some months resume conventional operations, hoping that world opinion, given the lack of definitive results from nuclear strikes, would persuade us to settle for less than our objective.

Also, some suggest that any U. S. use of nuclear weapons might trigger—immediately or eventually—a strike on the United States. Accordingly, they have linked our tactical nuclear posture with our strategic nuclear posture. In addition they further argue that use of nuclear weapons now could increase the chance that they might be used five or ten years from now in the Middle East or, in a moment of carelessness, in Europe. Accordingly, we should focus on strengthening the nuclear threshold by increasing our nonnuclear options. This argument is associated primarily with the early McNamara analysts in the Pentagon. More recently, analysts have looked seriously at a strong ABM system for the United States as a possible way of decoupling strategic and tactical nuclear weapons.

With respect to the third factor—worldwide reaction and consequences—the most serious is radioactivity. In Asia, a particular problem is presented by the prevailing winds, which are generally from the West. In Korea, for example, they tend towards Japan, and during a large part of the year they have a fairly high speed. A nuclear detonation in Korea could thus lead to radioactivity over Japan. Aside from these immediate effects, there would be radioactivity fallout around the world. For example, shots in the open would tend to push up the worldwide radioactivity level, even if they were small. Only so many weapons could be detonated without serious long term effects; otherwise in three to four years a critical level of, say, strontium 90 fallout would be reached.

Interrelating these "chess moves" is no easy problem. There has been a tendency at the analytic levels in Defense and elsewhere to look primarily at the first-order rounds of action and reaction, which are even in themselves not easy to formulate concisely, and not at the whole range of secondary consequences—whether the weapons will really work; what the specific military gains might be in using the weapons; what the full costs might be; what the real political and collateral effects might be; and particularly how the enemy might react. However, many of the Defense experts in thinking about nuclear weapons moved in 1969 from the Pentagon to the National Security Council staff and have been in a position to generate studies which pursue the issues in more detail. Thus the Nixon administration has a better chance to study and to cope with the issues of tactical nuclear war.

LEONARD RODBERG: Harold Agnew, the new director of Los Alamos Laboratory, has said that it is time to renew our examination of the use of tactical nuclear weapons. Would you comment on the relative mood now as compared to, say, five years ago within the military establishment on the role of tactical nuclear weapons?

STANLEY M. KANAROWSKI: Actually, aside from one or two projects, there has been very little development of these weapons in the last ten or fifteen years. Of course, Kennedy had attacked Eisenhower on the basis of a "missile gap," and in the early Kennedy years there was a great deal of focus on this problem. Even after it had been determined that the gap didn't exist, there were heavy procurements and heavy allocations of funds for strategic missiles. But this was done at the expense of other nuclear programs. At any rate, since 1960 there has been little development of tactical nuclear weapons. With respect to specific tactical doctrine for nuclear weapons in Asia, there has been even less. This is because for a long period of years, discussion has been focused on Europe. And there was a general feeling that what was determined for Europe applied anywhere else; because of techniques of analysis

—attrition rates and so forth—planners were relatively indifferent to the type of target.

MARCUS G. RASKIN: I wonder if there are initiatives within government to withdraw tactical nuclear weapons from Asia?

EARL C. RAVENAL: There are perennial initiatives within the Department of Defense for a variety of reasons, some of which you might find significant and some of which are merely technical: such as increased ability to reintroduce them, expense, obsolescence of certain types, reliance on even more massive means of destruction, changes in tactical doctrine, and so forth. There are several different kinds of reasons why initiatives of this sort are perennial.

Strategy and
the Evolution of 1½ Wars

EARL C. RAVENAL: The 1½ war strategy of the Nixon administration is integrally related to the new defense planning procedures discussed earlier by Pierre Sprey. It forms the general boundary of the "strategic guidance" for the defense program that is issued by the White House in conjunction with the "fiscal guidance." It certainly holds serious implications for our Asian policy. It might be appropriate here to relate certain observations I have of the early process of evolution of this new strategy and certain impressions I have derived from members of the Defense and National Security staffs of the factors that conditioned the results. Several main points are to be made.

1. Toward the end of the McNamara and Clifford regimes in the Defense Department, a serious disillusion had settled upon many defense planners—even the systems analysts— with regard to the existing model for deriving national security requirements. This model has been described by Pierre Sprey earlier in this conference. You will remember that it began as a requirements-oriented "buy-what-we-need" approach, and had become—in an effort to limit the excesses of this approach—a fixed force structure planning system. The fixed force structure approach itself bred certain kinds of excesses, in its turn. Notably, it led to "gold-plating" of each element of the force structure, to the development of expensive

multipurpose weapons systems, and in general to the cost-enhancement of every unit that was controlled in basic numbers but not in dollars. At the beginning of the incoming Nixon administration, therefore, there was a great receptivity to initiatives that had begun to develop within the Defense staff to install a fixed-budget model—to impose dollar ceilings on functional and administrative categories of the defense effort. The idea was to expose defense planning again to the shock of contact with the real world.

2. Literally on the first day the Nixon administration took office—January 20, 1969—prototype studies were presented, and full studies proposed, to examine a complete range of alternative force postures and defense budget levels both for strategic and general purpose forces. The general purpose alternatives included at least eight options, ranging from a Western hemisphere only strategy; to the defense of only one of the major theaters, Asia or Europe, totally writing off the other; to the defense of both theaters, but not simultaneously; to the existing 2½ war strategy; to a strategy including the simultaneous defense of both Southeast Asia and Korea; to variants that included active forces for a counterattack; to options that either did not count the contributions of many of our allies, or included them on the assumption of expanded military assistance. The full study of this wide range of options commanded the attention of many agencies of government for more than a year and provided perhaps the greatest theoretical political-military-economic education any incoming administration has ever received. But one point should be made: that serious practical attention was then limited to a few alternatives, lying in a narrow band around the existing one. None went beyond McNamara's planning premise of 2½ wars, and none went below 1½ wars.

LEONARD RODBERG: What happened to the strategy of planning to defend only the Western hemisphere?

EARL C. RAVENAL: The Western hemispheric strategy was never seriously considered. It was, apparently, discarded very early as not in the national interest. Incidentally, you might have noticed that Secretary Laird objected to the characterization "1½ war strategy." He said that we have a no-war strategy. This might not be as benign a statement as it sounds; it might well foreshadow a return to a deterrent posture.

3. A principal point is that the Nixon administration was never really talking about "strategies," as such. What it was really considering was alternative force levels and budgets. Rough strategic concepts were selected that would give some point and substance to the various force levels, but the basic effort was to size our military forces to arrive at budget planning factors. Dollar ceilings would be set, and the Services would be constrained to spend the money more wisely, it was thought, within the ceilings. As one national security planner described it to me:

> If you want to look at it realistically, a lot of analysis was done; and then President Nixon picked a strategy that suited his economic posture. On one side, he looked at his budget and said that he had only so much money to spend for defense. If he spent that much, he wouldn't have to fight with a lot of people, because everybody could see that he was constrained. On the other side, if he tried to arrive at even a lower level by more rational management, by better selection of weapons systems, and so on, he would run into other sorts of difficulties, such as unemployment. Obviously, President Nixon also chose a level that was politically comfortable; one of the things that would make him uncomfortable would be the feeling that he might choose too low a level and some catastrophe might occur: that China might suddenly invade Southeast Asia or Northeast Asia, or Russia invade Europe. As long as he felt that by reducing forces he was not running that kind of risk, then he could allow other factors to determine the level of forces.

4. Another point is that the budget level is threatened by inflation. The level of the fiscal year 1971 budget is probably representative of what defense budgets will be for the next few

years, in constant dollars. But the cost of both weapons systems and manpower is rising at a rate that even surpasses the general pace of inflation. For example, the average cost per man of pay, support, food, housing, and so on, now is in the neighborhood of $7,500 a year. According to projections, it will be $12,000 a year in about five years. The reason for this is that the Nixon administration is raising pay for the first two years of service. A volunteer army would cost another $3.5 billion a year over the next few years. And these increases are in addition to military pay increases in step with Federal General Service comparability formulas against the civilian sector. One of the things that the 1½ war strategy doesn't answer is how many men you need, because of the wide range of disagreement on how many forces are required for this strategy. So the economics of a fixed defense budget tend to determine defense manpower. Something has to be cut—either weapons systems of manpower, or both. All this points to well under 2.5 million men in the future, which is less manpower than we have had since the Eisenhower period.

RICHARD F. KAUFMAN: It sounds as if, when the question was raised whether to streamline the arsenal of weapons by reducing quantities and perhaps changing over to less costly systems, or reduce manpower, the decision was made to keep the weapons and let the people go.

EARL C. RAVENAL: In itself, the 1½ war strategy doesn't decide between manpower and weapons. The military will tell you they need so many divisions to carry out the strategy. Civilian analysts will say you need less. But nowhere does this discussion address the equipment modernization problem. The new strategy certainly does not strictly entail a high level of weapons systems, though that remains a probable trade-off that might well be adopted.

STANLEY M. KANAROWSKI: There are two points to be made here. First, when it came to the decision on the 1½ war strategy versus the 2½, there was a wide divergence between what the systems analysts felt was necessary for 2½ wars and what the Joint Chiefs of Staff felt: something like $75 million versus $100 million. But *both* figures were considerably over what Secretary Laird was willing to buy. Second, in the process of selling their study, the systems analysts stated that they weren't talking about the number of men or the question of carrier-based versus land-based aircraft.

RICHARD F. KAUFMAN: If we consider the 1½ war strategy in the context of the Nixon Doctrine, we can see that under the Nixon Doctrine, clearly the decision was made to reduce manpower levels in foreign countries but to increase the level of weapons in and around those same countries through military assistance. When we look at Southeast Asia, we see an increase in our fleet in the Pacific and an increase in airpower in that area.

EARL C. RAVENAL: I agree that the Nixon strategy implies greater reliance on allied forces in the military theaters, and this in turn implies vastly increased military assistance—grant aid, credit sales, straight sales, and the giving of excess U. S. equipment. But it need not imply an *overall* higher level of weapons systems in the theaters. We could just as well see a net depletion of strength, and this would also have implications that do not inspire confidence in future U. S. choices.

MILTON KOTLER: Did you say that if President Nixon chose a lower level, some people might think the Chinese could invade and we wouldn't be prepared? Are you saying that is the reason he didn't choose a still lower level?

EARL C. RAVENAL: My impression is that, on the contrary, he didn't choose a *higher* level because he didn't feel that he needed those forces to prevent those catastrophes; and one of the considerations in allowing a lower force level and a budget reduction was a *lack* of immediate concern that the reduction would be dangerous.

STANLEY M. KANAROWSKI: If I understand Mr. Kotler's question, it is: how low could we go *below* 1½? Here I think the people designing this study didn't want to take on another round of sensitive and complex negotiations with our European allies. We had just completed a set of negotiations at the time. It was originally part of the initiative to go lower in Europe, and then in the summer of 1968, when the study was being written, we had Czechoslovakia. Everybody was excited and it didn't seem timely to invest more talent in trying to make that option sound reasonable.

MILTON KOTLER: You say it could have been lower but for Czechoslovakia, which excited opinion in this country? In other words, you mean in terms of real strategic considerations it could have been lower, but for Czechoslovakia and public opinion, for which the government is responsible. The question remains, then: what is the *real* lower bound?

EARL C. RAVENAL: I think what emerges is that there is not a single factor, but a complexity of factors that prevented the serious consideration of lower bounds that might have occurred on strategic grounds alone. For this reason, one might call strategy "the dismal science," because the strategy-formation process is apparently so externally constrained that it is nearly impossible for any deliberate consideration to be given to a very low option.

MILTON KOTLER: That is a serious problem.

STANLEY M. KANAROWSKI: I would like to clarify one point. What was preserved was Europe, but not indefinitely. To take on Europe would have called for a round of negotiations. We have procedures that call for annual negotiations on force levels in Europe. To take on that task would have delayed implementation of the decisions. But President Nixon's policy statement says that we are going to analyze Europe; we are going to look at six or seven questions and then perhaps come up with a new strategy for Europe.

MARCUS G. RASKIN: I take it that, in order to keep the budget reasonably in balance, what they are going to do is attempt to end the draft and raise pay and pensions for soldiers. To what extent, I wonder, have they undertaken action which would up the budget and cause more commitments, in the hope that they would be able to cut other things—but the cutting of other things hasn't occurred?

EARL C. RAVENAL: Raising the budget doesn't necessarily mean that you are taking on more commitments; just as, unfortunately, cutting the budget does not mean reducing commitments. It may just mean buying more modernization, or eliminating low pay for people in the army in the first two years in an effort to induce more people to volunteer and consequently end the draft.

MARCUS G. RASKIN: If they raise the pay of a military grouping on the theory that the draft system is going to end, but in fact the draft system doesn't end, they will expand the amount of money for people in the military. They may have both simultaneously.

EARL C. RAVENAL: But they must have the money to do that. That is one point about fixed budget ceilings. With rising costs it is reasonable to project that under one assumption or another manpower will fall. It is the obvious place to cut.

MARCUS G. RASKIN: If the president and his staff are simply looking for a comfortable budget and operating within fixed ceilings, they will be less interested in stopping particular groupings which may insist on their piece of the action.

Politics,
Intervention, and Escalation

DANIEL ELLSBERG: As a student of the Vietnam war, I'd like to address the questions: what have we been up to in Vietnam over the last twenty years, and how does that bear upon what we are likely to be up to in Asia in the future?

As one gets into internal documentation, or as one gets as close to decision-making as I have been in certain years, one confronts some paradoxes and puzzles about the Vietnam war that are not troublesome to people who are limited to the public record. In public discussions, one finds the thesis that presidents have been led astray by their bureaucrats, or by their own wishful fantasies, to imagine that the steps they were taking in Vietnam from year to year, from 1950 on, were adequate in themselves to end the war, win the war, or prevent a communist takeover. The thesis goes that they were thus led to adopt a series of actually inadequate steps in escalation, led on by the momentum of past actions, in order to justify past actions.

This thesis is not validated by the internal record. Instead one confronts the fact that, for reasons we don't correctly know, presidents were led to take actions which their bureaucrats, both military and civilian, warned them year after year were not adequate to win the war, were costly, were risky in themselves, and would lead to the necessity of taking further actions which would be still more costly and risky. One gets a sense not of a wishful or—as Arthur Schlesinger would put it —"inadvertent" wandering into a quagmire, but rather of a desperate series of deliberate actions. One sees a succession of presidents wrestling with secret problems—secret in the sense that they did not share with the public the pessimistic vision that they were given by large parts of their bureaucracy at the time. This is another aspect of the curious pattern of behavior: the fact that presidents, except for brief periods, did not expose to the public the low probability of success. To be specific, I go back to the original aid to the French in the early fifties, the support in 1954 and 1955, the increase in advisory effort and other commitments in 1961, the participation in the coup against Diem in 1963, the initial bombing of North Vietnam in early 1965, the initial commitment of troops in the spring of 1965, and the open-ended commitment of troops in the summer of 1965 and continuing for some years thereafter. In not one of these cases were presidents led to believe that the steps they were taking would be adequate to gain their long-run objective: the securing of Vietnam from communist control.

So one has the image, not of a man with his mind on other things wandering into the quicksand and gradually finding himself mired, but of Eliza crossing the river, jumping from one block of ice to another as each slips beneath her feet. What was it that American presidents were fleeing so desperately in those moments of decision?

Of course, it is not the case that they were pessimistic at all points in time. There were periods of optimism; but the optimism always came *after* the decisions of escalation and as a *result,* bureaucratically and psychologically, of the steps of escalation. One is led to a hypothesis which has great significance for other decision-making in Asia, past and future. As one looks at the record and reflects on his own experience, one is struck by the similarity of the considerations brought to bear on each of the specific decisions, rather than their uniqueness. For instance, in the coup, the 1965 escalation, or the bombing, the stated interests, the prospects, the alternatives in each case seem remarkably similar. And that leads one to distrust any explanation of a particular decision which is highly specific to any particular period. One searches rather for the origins of the underlying attitudes and perceptions. Each time one looks at an earlier period one is dismayed at the thought of having tried to understand a later one without knowing the facts of the earlier one.

For example, in my opinion, the 1948 to 1954 period holds a large part of the answer to the question: what has been driving a succession of presidents? [1] The answer, very briefly, is that a certain faction of the Republican Party seized on the vulnerability of the Democratic administration that happened to be in office during the takeover of China by the communists. The result of that taught a generation of bureaucrats and politicians what could happen to an administration that happened to be in power when Indochina fell to the communists. To use Harold Isaacs's phrase, it created very deep scratches on the minds of politicians and bureaucrats. It pointed out the moral: do not lose Indochina while you are in office. Ideally, do not ever lose it, in the judgment of history. If that can't be achieved, at least do not display immediate responsibility for it by actually being in office when the event takes place. This gave a very high priority to short-run measures which would at least postpone the "loss" of Indochina or any part of the region to communism.

Another reason for the extreme emphasis on the short run was the apparent presidential suspicion, in line with intelligence estimates (though not with the proposals of some "operators"), that one could not, practically speaking, do better than that postponement; one couldn't secure the long-run future of that area without taking certain measures far beyond those a U. S. administration could take "safely," in the light of domestic political constraints. There was another proscription

1. As to why their efforts were doomed to be frustrated, the crucial history seems to be still earlier, in the 1945–1946 period in Vietnam.

which had its roots in the same period, thanks to the Korean war: Do not get involved in a land war in Asia. Do not commit ground troops to Asia. So presidents have been confronted, because of the fall of China, the events in Korea, the particular Republican response of that period, and the vulnerability then of the Democrats, with a dilemma: on the one hand the imperative "do not lose Indochina," and on the other hand the constraint "do not use ground troops to save it; do not even use air if you can avoid it; do not get militarily involved."

The first resolution of this dilemma is to give up the long-term aims and see what one can salvage. The answer has been that the president could usually salvage a noncommunist Saigon government for the short run. Intelligence estimates have assured the president from month to month and year to year that he could avoid losing Indochina *this year* if he was willing to pay the price; in fact, he could do it without using American troops, for a rather long time. If one reads the early intelligence estimates throughout the fifties, they would lead one to believe that by relying on allies—French or Vietnamese—assuring them that one will eventually come in when needed, giving them financial support and logistic support and air support and so forth, one could keep Indochina out of communist hands, keep Saigon out of communist hands, until about 1965; but then one would have to use troops. No estimate actually *said* that, but it is a reading that is consistent with what was actually said. If one looks at the predictions of how long the French could last in the face of the Vietminh, what the communists would probably do in response to Geneva, what they would do after 1956 when the elections were cancelled, one would conclude that it would not be until a few years before or after 1965 that one would have to use U. S. troops to keep Vietnam out of communist hands in the short run. But one can explain presidential actions without assuming that they ever had that eventual necessity clearly in mind. Rather they were driven from year to year by short-run constraints on what they could and could not get away with.

The trouble with this model is that it is a recursive formula: don't lose Vietnam *this year*. This takes you from year to year. Don't use troops until or unless you have to to prevent Vietnam from falling *this year*. Don't use planes, don't take risks with China and Russia, unless you have to to avoid losing it *this year,* or before the next congressional or presidential election. And that not only determines the policy; it explains many aspects of it. What it doesn't explain is where the process stops. It doesn't tell the president when to decide to lose Vietnam. It doesn't tell where the turning point is. Perhaps this is because there isn't any clear turning point in the nature of the situation. Or perhaps there will have to be a sharp change in the parameters of the system and a considerable transformation of the dynamics of the system before a president reaches a turning point and really does get out— that is, accepts the loss of Vietnam.

If we look ahead as far as 1976 and ask which of the intervening years would Richard Nixon decide to be a good year for him and the Republican Party to lose Indochina, no one year clearly emerges. Ironically, as one looks at year after year from 1950 on, some years are less bad than others. Sixty-one was a particularly bad year for the Democrats to lose Indochina, after the Bay of Pigs and the Berlin Wall. Although we had a new president, with less ideology than some others, that was a bad year. Other years were less bad. Sixty-nine looked from many points of view like one of the most painless years for losing Indochina that any president has confronted. But for a number of reasons, one of which is that the president was Richard Nixon, we didn't choose that year. Seventy is not much easier than any of the other years, nor is 1971. So we are back on the old track.

Even in years when it would have been politically less costly to get out, it would have been hard ideologically for Richard Nixon, who was very much "present at the creation" (though Acheson, who coined that title, was looking more at Europe and is very modest about his actual midwifery role in Indochina). Of course, our policy did not start in 1953; it did not start under the Republicans; it started under Acheson and Truman in 1949 and 1950 and shows no great change in any subsequent year. So in Richard Nixon we have a president who in 1950 was one of the hounds at the backs of the Democrats, who knows just what would be said and done if he were to falter with respect to Indochina as Truman faltered with respect to China. He knows it because he once ran with the hounds. He would almost envy the position of one who would try to bring him down on a charge of treason, weakness, or softness on communism. In fact, if you were to ask which role he would rather have, psychologically, Nixon's after losing Indochina or Reagan's, setting out to bring him down, there would be no question. So Nixon doesn't envision himself deliberately losing Indochina this year, next year, or any other year.

In fact, the Nixon Doctrine itself exhibits many of the characteristics of the dilemma that confronted Democratic politicians in 1949 and 1950. You can't read a word on the fall of China and the McCarthy period without feeling that you are reading current events. There was a combination of doctrines put forward by the "Asia First" group, somewhat curiously called by Norman Graebner the "New Isolationists" (I understand this term was first applied by Arthur Schlesinger, Jr.), though they were really for intervention in Asia, because they had the same political base as the pre-World War II isolationists. The older isolationists, too, though essentially isolationists vis-à-vis Europe, never had the same inhibitions about intervention in Asia; there was always this irony in the label. In any case, these people believed that Asia was of extreme importance to the United States and was threatened by a communist takeover. The loss of Asia would be extremely costly to the United States, but this fate could be prevented relatively cheaply by a patriotic and resolute administration which neither harbored traitors within its midst nor shrank from backing up its threats with air power and, if necessary, nuclear weapons. There was another element: a willingness to use Asian allies. If we were willing to rely on Korea, nationalist China, and other allies, and back them up with the threat of U. S. air power, there was no need to lose. So deterrence should work, and if deterrence didn't work, you carried out your air threats. This was a fully developed model.

Certain basic premises were implicit in the critique of the fall of China which implied that either treason or total incompetence had to be involved. One is that without putting land armies in China—which no one suggested—we could have "easily" avoided this defeat. This was quickly followed by the MacArthur critique of our policies in Korea: the idea that a willingness to bomb China, to use nuclear weapons if necessary, could have avoided our problems in Asia.

Experience shows that this thesis has the potential of mobilizing a considerable part of U. S. opinion in moments of doubt and crisis. In sum, a president will be subject to punishment from the Asia-first right wing if he loses an area to communism. He will also be punished, by them along with many others, if he invests too much in preventing the loss. And if intelligence analyses say that we can't avoid losing in the short run without investing a good deal of money and effort, and if a president cannot get even this much aid from Congress if he were to tell Congress that all he is doing is postponing the loss until next November, the only way to resolve this is to tell Congress that he is asking for this much because it *will* be enough. He must lie about his own intelligence analyses and cross his fingers. He must hope that he can play the same game with Congress when the next installment comes due. That expectation has turned out very well, in fact, year after year.

Now with the Nixon Doctrine, for the first time since Eisenhower we are hearing again about Asian allies, U. S. air power, and, it may yet turn out, reliance on nuclear weapons.

With the same budgetary pressures that led to an increasing re-liance on nuclear weapons in the New Look period in the fifties—a reliance which Nixon defended publicly at the time and showed no reservations about—we could again, given the maintenance of all our commitments about holding on to Asia and keeping it out of communist hands, see the reinstatement of such policies. And that does not add up to disengagement. There are so many items of contradiction in our present Asian policy—not just in the rhetoric—that it would be a strange characterization of it to call it disengagement. I, for one, would say that it doesn't look anything like disengagement; it looks rather like "escalation when necessary." Within the next several years, escalation is to be expected, I would say, in In-dochina. The same thing applies elsewhere in Asia.

I may close with a puzzle that I have not resolved in my own mind: where does the "Asia First" doctrine come from —that is, the notion that U. S. "security" and national inter-ests depend as much or even more on events and politics in Asia as in Europe? How do Americans get themselves into the state of mind that it is crucially important to American inter-ests, or to their own interests, whether communists run various parts of Asia or not? Why does it come to be of such tran-scendent importance that we are motivated to take major risks to prevent it? Why did the "Asia First" group of Senators and others feel this way? Why did they get such a response from the American public? Would they still get it today? To what extent have presidents feared this approach in others? To what ex-tent have they actually shared it? If presidents have shared that view, why have they?

As long as presidents are led to believe that they will be in bad trouble from the American public if they are responsible for losing parts of Asia to communism, they will engage us in extremely risky and costly efforts when they think it neces-sary. There may be other reasons, but that alone would be compelling. I conclude reluctantly that we have elected and have been led by presidents who, whatever the other reasons they may have had, were willing to kill large numbers of Asians, destroy Asian societies, imperil American society, and sacrifice large numbers of Americans from time to time, mainly for the reason that their party and they themselves would be in political trouble if they did not. That is a very serious charge. If it is true, and if our future presidents are like our past, then we face a future not of disengagement, but of continued involvement and intervention, a future not of peace but of greater war than we have seen in the past in Asia.

FRANZ SCHURMANN: What Mr. Ellsberg said about being locked into a foreign policy is something I would subscribe to very strongly. Something is needed to break out of the system, the system being the logic of this Southeast Asia policy that dates back to the late forties and perhaps even back to the thirties. I assume that there may be elements in the U. S. government—whether in the "New State Department in the White House" or in other departments—that want to reduce our commitments or change the nature of our commitments in Southeast Asia, either because they cost too much or because there may be more urgent problems abroad. Is there some thinking, conscious or unconscious, that a crisis in the Middle East—not only in terms of American commitment to Israel or America's interests in the Arab world, but in terms of an arms race with the Soviet Union—might serve as a context in which one could break out of the logic of Southeast Asia?

DANIEL ELLSBERG: I take it you are referring to Secretary Rogers and perhaps Secretary Laird. I would certainly not make that inference about President Nixon. The debate over American interests in Southeast Asia throughout the decade has not been about the importance either domestically or strategically to the U. S. of that area, but about the means by which one safeguards these interests. On the one hand you use alliances plus U. S. air and nuclear power, and on the other hand you use alliances plus U. S. ground troops, with a strong attempt to get away from reliance on nuclears—which was the policy of the New Frontier in 1961. You are suggesting that Secretary Rogers and Secretary Laird might go further than that and downgrade U. S. interests in that area. I cannot discern that they would be very influential if they were to suggest this within the administration. So I would not guess that Middle East policy is being manipulated with a view to covering a true disengagement in Asia.

FRANZ SCHURMANN: I was paraphrasing a line in a book by Anthony Downs, called *Inside Bureaucracy*. He says there is no way to change an existing agency. If you want to get a new program through, you must create a new agency, and then you have the force to change the original agency.

DANIEL ELLSBERG: If I thought the president really wanted to get out of Southeast Asia, I could entertain the notion that a crisis in the Middle East might appear as an opportunity.

MILTON KOTLER: When you speak of the perpetuation of escalation as a refusal to admit defeat, doesn't this mean the consequence of increasing guilt? Aren't you alluding to a psychology of guilt—a passion, or love, of guilt that feeds on itself? It starts with not wishing to terminate the war for political reasons and ends with killing an Asian society.

DANIEL ELLSBERG: I think that is a fair question. But it is not evident to me that guilt is a predominant psychological consequence of this policy. First of all, many people in the Nixon administration do not perceive themselves as responding to the motives which an observer sees; and second, even in those moments when they do—moments of crisis when they may become relatively conscious—they would not see their choices as wrong or illegitimate. They need both of those perceptions to conclude that they should feel guilty.

MILTON KOTLER: Why is the consciousness of guilt absent?

DANIEL ELLSBERG: Surely these things are in part matters of their cultural values, validated not only by their own consciousness but by the responses of people around them. The fact is that these people do not travel in circles which would give them the impression that they are doing something illegitimate, inexcusable, if in fact they commit the lives of Americans and kill other people for such purposes. There is enough feeling that they might be questioned to lead to a certain amount of secrecy, and you could take secrecy as an indication of guilt, if you believed that presidents and other people in an administration only kept secrets when they had a terrible compulsion to do so. I think, however, that they will keep secrets if there is even a slight convenience in doing so. They will lie whenever it is slightly convenient to do so. So we can't infer from lies and secrets that they feel guilty.

MILTON KOTLER: If a president is conscious that what is at stake is only his political future, then he should be conscious also of the disproportion between that stake and the enormity of the crime.

DANIEL ELLSBERG: People on the inside—not only presidents, but people who serve presidents—protect themselves by a great variety of devices. Some are more sincere than others. They do this possibly to ward off the consciousness that they are acting primarily for political reasons. When I say political reasons, I don't mean only reelection but the position of a party in elections beyond the current one, one's place in history, the ability to govern, and other political considerations. What I have said would make very angry, and perhaps honestly angry, people like Rostow, Rusk, McNamara, Johnson, and Kennedy. To the extent that this is sincere self-deception, it is a shield against guilt: "I am acting for much more legitimate reasons." They certainly take great pains to convince others of that and to a large extent convince themselves.

LEONARD RODBERG: One of the ways they perhaps shield themselves from guilt is by persuading themselves that they are really taking the hard course. Nixon keeps saying the easy way would be to pull out. Johnson used the same rhetoric. And probably the rhetoric they use in the public context is the same rhetoric they use privately. So they see themselves as making a great sacrifice by sticking with it day in and day out, reading the casualties and struggling on, and not as having taken the easy way out.

International Order
and American Behavior

MARCUS G. RASKIN: The polemics of foreign policy
debate have their own ironies. Let me give you an example.
Since the American disenchantment with the Vietnam war,
liberals, radicals, and revisionists have had a chance to explore in the media major questions of foreign policy which
ordinarily would have been limited to little magazines and
limited-circulation books. But as a result of the Vietnam
nightmare-adventure, the managers of American foreign policy (whether in or out of the government) have lost their
sense of certitude and, as even President Nixon has pointed
out, have lost the will to design grand policy or plan grand
or even little wars. This means that now many ideas can be
debated at least without suffering the supercilious smirk of
the Establishment.

But the foreign policy managers have not abandoned their
dogma of "internationalism." They protect themselves by at-
tacking as "isolationist" all those who question the very basic
assumptions of American foreign and national security policy.
This term of supposed opprobrium is applied to anyone who
questions or opposes the pact system (NATO, SEATO,
CENTO, ANZUS, etc.), the macabre charade of disarmament
and arms limitation talks, American military interventions,
the client-state method, brushfire war, nuclear war, or other
devices invented by an unaccountable executive and his bu-

reaucracy. The term isolationist has been used to describe, in short, anyone who fundamentally questions an inhuman, immoral, or imperial role of the United States in the world.

But of course that whole attack is against a straw man. There is hardly anyone in the United States who favors—or indeed can imagine—isolation from the world. There are very few, if any, of those who oppose nuclear war, the pact system, the negotiation of panache arms control agreements, and the unilateral manipulation of trade arrangements, who do not favor the idea of Americans cooperating with non-Americans, trading with them, traveling with them, talking and learning from them, and vice versa.

On the contrary—ironically—throughout the cold war period it has been the "internationalists" who have attempted to cut the American people off, by commercial, travel, and diplomatic restrictions, from any contact with China or Eastern Europe. The "internationalists" attempted—but failed—to limit American involvement in the world through administrative restrictions and "free world" rhetoric, and through the "loyalty baiting" by which many Americans can be intimidated, possibly because of their foreign ancestry.

Some might question this view, citing the seemingly extraordinary effort which Americans put forward in developing a new international structure at the end of World War II. What was that internationalist energy about? The short answer is that the American concept of the international order has been a United Nations structure in which the United States would operate according to two principles: (a) it would play within the rules, but (b) it would define the rules.

To comprehend the present international system of security, it is useful to sketch briefly some characteristics of the balance of power system as it developed after the Peace of Westphalia in 1648. The balance of power idea was predicated on a social structure in which there were ruling elites in each country who bequeathed power from one generation to another and were related to each other by blood, religion, and class. In

Europe these groups of people intermarried dynastically, were supported by the Church, and were strengthened by the idea of the divine right of kings. Later these ruling groups were stabilized by the economic power of the bourgeoisie. They controlled the destinies, and particularly the foreign policies, of European states. From time to time ruling families intermarried, strengthening bonds of friendship—though, as in all families, causing complications—and constraining wars so they would not undercut the power of ruling elites similar to themselves. In many cases these groups borrowed from the same banks, whether the Fuggers, the Rothschilds, or the Morgans. The balance of power system included a formal and informal structure of communication in which limits were easily found and set because the values of the players were essentially the same. It also implied a method of resolving disputes in the context of limited wars and limited goals.

The advent of democracies upset the autocratic version of the balance of power system. Once governing was expanded to the bourgeoisie and to groups that were elected, by accident or persuasion, and did not necessarily hold the same interests as those who inherited their power—or powerlessness—new ruling elites and more unruly groups of people entered the game of international politics—though these unruly governing groups were regulated to some extent by their bureaucracies, which tended to set longer-term interests, purposes, and rules.

In 1917 the United States, having just finished fighting Mexico, undertook its first crusade in Europe. At the end of the war, Americans were entreated to join the League of Nations, a new Holy Alliance which would balance the power interests of the world according to the purposes of Europe. Historically, the original American ideal conception of the League of Nations was finally achieved—but not, as most people think, in the United Nations, although many of the League's specialized agencies with their bureaucratic shells carried over to 1945 and were incorporated in the United Nations structure. Rather, to American statesmen, the successor to the League was NATO. Here the basic groupings within the "West" could work together in various forms of collective defense under the hegemony of the United States.

So, in effect, the new imperial view was that Americans would (with the advice of the West Europeans) bring their own rule of law to the world. American statesmen would make the law to do what they wanted, and expand power and dominion through various modes of political, economic, and cultural penetration. When the surface was scratched, there was not to be law or cooperation in a truly international sense. Instead there was to be an exclusive system of dependencies and pacts which split the world. The dependency of the governments of Africa, Asia, or Latin America did not help their peoples. The economies and societies of these nations were disturbed, and the people—not the oligarchic rulers, whether they were communists or "free worlders"—suffered. The stance adopted internationally also caused the situation in Eastern Europe to be one of continuous tension and economic hardship.

Under the guise of internationalism, which fooled no one except the "educated," the United Nations was treated by the U. S. government as a front for its own purposes. When that no longer worked, the United Nations was dropped as an instrument of American foreign policy, though lip service was still paid to it, to assuage that part of the liberal and media communities which saw the United Nations as an important mechanism for peace.

What is clear, however, is that the United Nations could again emerge as an important unit of world organization. This might happen for several reasons. One is that China will enter the United Nations, with American acquiescence. (The reason for the acquiescence has less to do with China than it does with Japan. Various people within the American business and the bureaucratic community see Japan as a new threat to the United States—at least on the economic side. China becomes a new market for the United States and a military counterpoise to Japan and Russia.)

People are also reassessing the meaning of international co-operation. Such cooperation, if it is to mean more than un-realistic utopianism, must take account of the basic trans-formations in the world. For some elites there has been a greater possibility of travel and communication as a result of technological changes. This could mean a new exchange of ideas and understandings of what is going on in the world. Furthermore, there is a greater recognition of the fact that the vast majority of mankind is manipulated by forces which it does not know exist, let alone understand. In the United States this recognition comes at a time when the very definition of citizenship is under scrutiny. It would be well to say a few words about the implications of this problem for international relations.

International relations, historically, has been predicated on the existence of nation states comprised of citizens. Whether rich or poor, the citizen was tied by land and blood to his country. But the new consciousness in the world is forcing a very different sense of the meaning of citizenship. In the United States various groups, ethnic and otherwise, have begun to find that they have less in common with other groups of "fellow citizens"—especially ruling elites—than they have with the struggles and ideals of people outside the nation. This can be seen culturally as well as politically. Muhammad Ali expressed this thought when he said "no Viet Cong ever called me nigger." On the other hand, American foreign pol-icy is still conducted on the premise that the blacks in the ghettos have more in common with J. Edgar Hoover than they do with the Cuban revolutionaries.[1] The idea that citi-zenship could cover up class differences is breaking down. There is no longer a way to hold that the interests of the Mis-sissippi tenant farmer are the same as those of Rockefeller, or

1. Besides those who doubt their citizenship, others attempt to assert it in new ways. Recently college students have challenged their parents and the government by signing a "separate peace treaty" with the NLF and the North Vietnamese at a time when the official foreign policy continues to be defined in terms of war.

the interests of the draftee the same as those of the general. The genius of America—to assert and attempt to live that point of view within limits—has failed. The condition necessary for the flourishing of this view was that the U. S. would limit its activities as a great warrior power. Once war was not eschewed, but instead courted, our society split itself into class, race, and generational divisions that necessitate an entirely different foreign policy and call into question the entire notion of citizenship.

The American imperial system is failing. As is the case in such situations, new groups attempt to impress upon the situation their point of view and their own consciousness of what is necessary. The groups of people within the United States and elsewhere who have a fundamental stake in developing a new form of international cooperation will not sit idly by while the few divide up the rights of the many.

How does this new motion begin to show itself in international affairs? Let me mention several points as if to propose a program for international cooperation. Cooperation will have to be with and for the many, not the few. This means quite a different relationship with the mass of humanity than we have through the present state structure. It means active diplomatic relations and transnational relationships with the Chinese in mainland China. It means the development of new forms of direct and mutual aid between cities of the world— not mediated through national structures. Simultaneously, it requires that war preparation and warmaking be made a crime and that all nations develop the Nuremberg standards and make individuals liable as criminals for war preparations. Within the United States, officials of the government would be accessible as individuals to charges of high crimes under the Constitution. Such a standard, once it was adopted within the United States, would be pressed within a universal United Nations.

I see six major needs of a serious internationalism which would not assume the mantle of imperialism. These needs are already understood existentially by various groups in the United States who have come to political consciousness in the 1960s.

1. *Disarmament*. While this topic has—unjustly—become tedious, it *is* time that we began to disarm. One horrible problem of the Vietnam war has been that it has taken our minds and energies away from the arms race, which defies the parochialism of ideology. The United States could begin by ridding itself of more than 95 percent of its strategic and tactical weapons and still have enough to destroy the world's major population centers. It would be useful in this regard to initiate a transnational conference on disarmament, including scientists, students, and workers, which would be held for the specific purpose of developing immediate ways to rid ourselves of the curse of arms.

2. *Transnational arrangements*. It is no longer possible to talk of the nation state as the only player in world politics. It is to everyone's advantage to develop new loci of power and loyalty which would shake the foundations of the nation state and the psychological hold which state governments use as instruments to manipulate the poor and the wretched, and even the rich.

3. *Development of tax sharing concepts*. It is crucial that new forms of taxation be devised which would allow for international sharing. Such sharing would be used for projects chosen by the recipient nation. It would be allocated through regional groups of states and people, responsive to an international plan for world development that embodied the protection of cultural diversity.

4. *Cancellation of debt*. The United States should cancel all debts which are now owing to it under its military and foreign assistance arrangements. Such loans should have been grants in the first place. They have become drags on other countries and distort the possibility of constructive revolutionary progress.

5. *Development of international means of communication*

—attempts to use television, radio, etc., to bring people closer together without destroying the culture of the hearer and viewer.

6. *United Nations revision*—charter review which would reflect the changing realities which I have discussed.

Implementation of these needs would be the condition and the foundation of a new international order. The attempt to brand this kind of program "isolationist" is the current absurdity—if not the obscenity—of the proponents of the old and distorted internationalism, which is nothing but the perpetuation of imperialism in the guise of concern for the world.

National Budgets
and Major Choices

CHARLES P. SHIRKEY: I think it is important to bring the discussion into focus. I want to concentrate on the practical consequences of policy options for Asia as they might be seen from the White House perspective. That perspective, and the decision framework and mechanisms that are operative at the level, are the factors that make a difference in the real world. And my comments might further support a judgment that the process of getting from here to there is perhaps more relevant than the question of where "there" is. I am concerned here more with the process and factors of choice than with the particular budget figures and the defense policy they suggest for fiscal year 1971, 1972, or any future year.

The inescapable fact is that defense costs billions of dollars, and implementation of current defense policies in East Asia accounts for a large portion of that. This makes a discussion of alternatives in East Asia focus on a combination of political and budgetary considerations.

The alternatives, whatever they might be, to our current policies in East Asia will be hammered out in a process in which we might look at the political objectives and constraints as the "anvil," and the budget process as the "hammer." What gets hammered out are the programs and policies themselves. Following this analogy, I would suggest that the timing and the force of the budget hammer is critical. In the bureaucracy it is referred to as the "budget crunch."

Assuming the president's political antennae and policy objectives are established, the political anvil in this analogy is more or less a given. However, what the president and the administration must assess every year is the budget hammer. Usually each summer the president's economic advisors make an assessment of the next fiscal year's receipts based on GNP and growth rate projections. Estimates are also made for expenditure increases, given the current fiscal year program, for workload changes, the timing of obligations, and the nature of the legislation. The administration differentiates between that portion which is relatively uncontrollable and accounts for more than half of the total budget, such as Medicare and interest on the national debt, and so-called controllable programs, the biggest of which is the defense budget. Finally, both receipts and outlays are subjected to assumptions about inflation. The result is the first approximation of the next year's budget: the size of the deficit or surplus; the size of the fiscal dividend (if any) for new programs; and the amount that has to be cut from existing programs in real terms, and the relative priorities for doing so. This first approximation, which becomes guidance for the administration's planners, depends on the president's economic and political philosophy. Thus, in form and substance it is truly a White House perspective.

Taking the fiscal year 1972 budget as a relevant and timely example, the president is confronted with about $82 billion of defense spending—taking the fiscal year 1971 budget levels and projecting them with inflation, modernization cost increases, and pay increases. Overall, he is looking at a potential $12 billion budget deficit, and certain assumptions can easily increase that to $15 to $18 billion or more. With this budget deficit and the current economic environment, the president is confronted with one of the most fundamental aspects of the "budget crunch." A great deal is beyond his control. In short, he has limited choices that represent variables he can influence to differing degrees and programs he can alter. One would be inflation: he could simply "finance" the deficit, at least in part. This would depend upon his economic philosophy. He also must take into account the estimated increases in uncontrollable outlays, far greater than had been anticipated or has been the pattern to date. Certainly, he would want to preserve some flexibility in the control of civilian expenditures, for political reasons alone. This leaves defense spending, which includes several variables. One is the process of Vietnamization. Here he is caught in somewhat of a dilemma: as he withdraws United States forces, he has to compensate with increased economic and military aid in order to stabilize the Vietnamese economy and subsidize the South Vietnamese army (ARVN). Another variable is the extent to which he can pull forces out of Korea, in the light of any commitment he might have made to Korea on the rate and conditions of withdrawal. There is also the Strategic Arms Limitation Talks (SALT), and its possible impact on spending, or at least on the timing of spending, for ABM and such other strategic programs as the B-1 strategic bomber and the Undersea Long-range Missile System (ULMS). The forces deployed and committed to NATO do not appear to be regarded by the Nixon administration as alterable at this time.

Against these variables, which represent options, the president is also looking at risks and confidence levels. The bureaucratic process is very important in this regard, because this process presents the alternatives, and indeed attempts to assess for the president the risks and costs, not only from a dollar standpoint, but also from a political and security standpoint. For example, the president is concerned about the impact of any moves upon our allies. He is concerned about how the timing of withdrawal and disengagement measures might affect Korea, Thailand, and perhaps most important Japan. He is also concerned about how these moves might be perceived on the other side: by the Chinese, Soviets, and North Vietnamese.

There are certain trade-off options that he has among programs and budgets. One is the trade-off between military assistance and U. S. forces. This mix of self-defense capability, complemented by certain U. S. forces as needed, is critical to the implementation of the Nixon Doctrine in East Asia. Of the $3.5 billion in world-wide security assistance outlays today, I would suggest that as much as $3–3.2 billion could be used as a trade-off or alternative to far more costly U. S. conventional forces.

But the extent to which there is a trade-off, namely, the extent to which allied forces can be used to meet *U. S.* objectives at acceptable confidence levels against U. S. perceived threats and satisfy U. S. commitments, is not well understood, even within the administration. For example, we don't know precisely to what extent our withdrawal and disengagement from East Asia can be compensated by increased expenditures or a different mix of expenditures on allied forces in order to arrive at the same U. S. confidence levels in the political and territorial integrity of these countries. We don't know what it takes in terms of the total cost; however, we are fairly confident that greater allied participation will cost less than primary reliance on U. S. forces. However, we are not sure of the economic, social, and political constraints which will limit the effectiveness, if not the desirability, of increased assistance. It is abundantly clear, for example, that South Vietnam cannot, after U. S. withdrawal, operate the large ARVN forces we have created without continued large U. S. outlays to subsidize these forces. And we do not thoroughly understand how, in strict military terms, these forces might be used to complement one another in various types of contingencies in the form of collective security. For example, to what extent can various indigenous forces in East Asia be used in a regional role? Will Filipino forces or Indonesian forces assist in Northeast or Southeast Asian contingencies? It is worth noting that most of the allied forces fighting in Vietnam are in effect mercenaries bought and paid for by the U. S. The Australian and New Zealand forces joined the fray only after considerable diplomatic pressure.

If self defense and collective security prove to be politically and militarily unattainable at any cost, the U. S. could further explore the trade-off of forces in East Asia for an increase in our airlift and sealift capability. But no one should accept the illusion that this is a cheaper alternative than the current posture. Moreover, there are some uncertainties in providing the necessary resources; the essential sealift component, for example, has never gotten off the ground.

In the context of budget pressures and the attempt to maximize confidence and minimize costs, there are some fundamental unanswered questions. From a defense standpoint there is a lot more analysis to be done on several points. If we look at the defense budget now and compare it with fiscal year 1969 as a base point, we might ask how much confidence we now have to meet the major contingencies, in Europe and East Asia. Recall that in fiscal year 1969 the U. S. accounted for 40 percent of the world's military spending: roughly $80 billion out of a worldwide total of some $200 billion. NATO as a whole was spending about $100 billion excluding the incremental costs of the Vietnam war.[1] At the same time, the Warsaw Pact was spending about $65 billion. This alone might suggest that we ought to have good confidence in our capability to deter, if not defend, in any reasonable set of contingencies. Of course, a large portion of our conventional forces in fiscal year 1969 were tied down in Vietnam. Even so, if we look simply at the forces we had at that time, and at the most demanding defense case should deterrence fail—which would be an all-out conventional war against the Soviets beginning in NATO—we might find that we had enough forces to give the president and the alliance the capability for "flexible response" without initial (and one would hope even ultimate) recourse to nuclear weapons.

1. The incremental cost of the Vietnam war is estimated at about $21 billion in fiscal year 1969.

Now if we start with that as an assumption, and take our forces out of Korea and Vietnam, and simply delete them from the force structure, we would end up with about 9⅓ active army divisions plus 3 active Marine divisions, about 25 active tactical air wings—maintaining the approximate two-to-one ratio of tactical air wings to divisions which we have kept virtually intact since the Second World War—and about 10 aircraft carriers. This would save about $13 billion a year if we got *all* the forces out of Vietnam and Korea, and had the managerial skill to identify and delete *all* the indirect support and administrative overhead that is associated with these forces. So on this set of assumptions we could save about $14 billion in 1972 dollars. And this would keep intact a flexible or graduated response in NATO or East Asia but not simultaneously.

But what if we change these assumptions—and that could be mostly a matter of different *timing* rather than substantive changes in defense policy *per se?* What if we assume certain constraints in the timing of Vietnam withdrawals; certain decisions the Nixon administration may arrive at in terms of residual forces in Vietnam; a different timing of withdrawals from Korea; and a different basis for calculating security assistance to our East Asian allies for self defense, collective security, and ultimately the replacement of U. S. forces? All these considerations, plus the budget crunch which will be felt in fiscal year 1972, will pose critical problems and questions, and in turn demand difficult decisions.

But budgets tend to have far-reaching effects in terms of the weapons systems we develop and procure, the forces we operate, and the readiness and deployability of these forces. The main defense policy questions are the collective effect of these decisions on our capability and, perhaps most important, our confidence in flexible response, first in NATO but also in Asia. In defense planning, regardless of whether the planning assumption is for 2½ wars or 1½ wars simultaneously, we are talking about an envelope in which we build forces to meet a range of contingencies. If we were to make further reductions in our NATO capability, either by withdrawing forces from NATO or reducing reserve forces in the continental United States, we would then raise questions about our conventional response and our reliance on nuclear weapons: in the first instance, tactical nuclear weapons; in the second instance, strategic nuclear weapons. And we still do not thoroughly understand the role and effectiveness of tactical nuclear weapons, either for fighting a war or as a deterrent prior to any sort of military engagement. Also, we are not sure about the types of contingencies we might encounter in Asia concurrent with a contingency in NATO. And this raises further questions with regard to the mix of forces—the number and type of divisions, the number and type of tactical air forces, the number of aircraft carriers, the sort of ASW (antisubmarine warfare) forces we retain, and of course the size and mix of allied forces.

What this amounts to is the basic defense policy question confronting the Nixon administration: do we retain flexible response in the 1970s, and if so how do we define it? To some extent we can address this question technically and in strict military and budgetary terms. But in the final analysis, it translates into a judgmental and political question: how much flexibility do we want the president to have in responding to contingencies before being forced into the dilemma of going nuclear or capitulating? In short, how much conventional capability are we prepared to buy and maintain, even if it is a mix of U. S. and U. S.-supported allied forces? I submit that question will be with us in the 1970s, as it was with us in the 1960s.

In closing, I would suggest there are some broader questions that force us even to redefine the meaning of national security and the means to ensure it. What are the *real* challenges to our national and global security in the 1970s? Admittedly, the problems of aggression and the tyranny of war are not likely to disappear. These problems have a very legitimate claim on our national resources. But there are also the problems of population growth, which has only been deferred a decade or two, thanks to the "green revolution"; economic and social deterioration, not only in the underdeveloped world, but also in the developed world; the adequacy of technology to cope with pollution, given the degree to which we are flagrantly abusing the world environment; and the potentially explosive issue of U. S. (and other developed countries') consumption of the world's resources, now 40 percent and predicted to be somewhere around 60 percent by the turn of the century. These are not just matters of national priorities; they are also matters of national *security* now and in the remaining decades of this century. In this sense the Nixon administration is correct when it states that we will solve both the problems at home and abroad or we will solve neither.

IV

THE ECONOMIC STAKES:
PROFITS OR LOSSES?

The Costs and
Benefits of Asia

RICHARD F. KAUFMAN: By some quirk of intellectual fashion it has become unseasonal, even vulgar, in some circles to speak seriously of economic influences on U. S. foreign policy. The war in Vietnam is seen by many observers as a refutation of Marxist and other orthodox indictments of the capitalistic tendency towards imperial expansion. The costs of Vietnam, it is argued, far exceed any potential economic gain that might accrue to the U. S., assuming even the most favorable conclusion of that miserable conflict; American business interests, it is maintained, do not have the magnitude of trade or investment interests in Vietnam that would explain away the enormous government outlays for the war. The considerable opposition to the war by businessmen appears to support the view that the causes of the war are psychological and political,[1] not economic.

For the most part, critics of the economic view of American foreign policy have erred in their bookkeeping and misconceived the problem. It is true that the U. S. as a whole can

---

1. Seymour Melman places responsibility for the war on the "institutionalized power-lust" of the Department of Defense. See Melman's *Pentagon Capitalism* (New York: McGraw-Hill, 1970), p. 4. For an earlier discription of America's role in the world as imperial although nonimperialistic, grounded on the responsibility to maintain world order through police operations such as the war in Vietnam, see George Liska, *Imperial America* (Baltimore: John Hopkins Press, 1967).

hope for no net economic gains from our investment in Vietnam. This, however, is usually the case in modern times. Vietnam does not resemble the wars that have been fought for territorial conquest in the classical sense, as a result of which whole nations, perhaps, prospered at the expense of the defeated. But, to take a narrow view of war for a moment, the fact is that the economic interests of particular groups and individuals are always advanced by international conflict. The questions, then, are *whose* interests are advanced by the foreign policy at hand, and what influence do they exert on the decision-making process?

Suppose, to take a not-so-hypothetical example, that $120 billion of government outlays will be required to fight a war in a small underdeveloped country. The known deposits of minerals and other sources of raw material are inconsequential. The potential market for U. S. exports is slight. Continued expenditures will probably be necessary to support a residual force to preserve a Korean-type settlement of the war. A gimlet-eyed cost accountant might find that economically such a war would be a losing proposition for the U. S. If he were auditing the books while the war was in progress, he would no doubt conclude that the decision to go into this war must have been dictated without regard to whether the nation would profit from its investment.

But what if our political CPA balanced not the national interest against the costs of the war, but rather the interests of a specific group of corporations, a handful of military leaders, and a number of civilian bureaucrats against those costs? As Gabriel Kolko has argued, "American interests in a country or region have often defined the national interest on the assumption that the nation can identify its welfare with the profits of some of its citizens—whether in oil, cotton, or bananas." [2] Vietnam is not noted for its oil, cotton, or bananas—although

2. Gabriel Kolko, *The Roots of American Foreign Policy* (Boston: Beacon, 1970), pp. 84–85.

there has been more than a hint of rich offshore oil deposits.[3] But U. S. spending for the war has itself produced a bountiful harvest for defense contractors. The defense budget increase from \$47 billion in 1965, on the eve of the Vietnam buildup, to about \$80 billion in 1969, during the peak war year, was in large part driven by defense contracts. During the same period, prime contract awards went from \$28 billion to \$44.6 billion.

Roughly half of total Vietnam outlays, \$60 billion, has gone to defense contractors to procure the hardware and services necessary for the war effort. What influence have the war contractors exerted on the decision to enter the war, the decision to escalate and pursue the war, or on our Asian foreign

3. According to the June 1970 issue of *Petroleum Engineer,* "if and when the U. S. wins its objectives there [in Vietnam], oil exploration conceivably could be successful enough to turn that part of the world into another Southern Louisiana, Texas type producing area."

Off-shore deposits have been suspected in the entire East Asia region, from the coasts of Burma to the coasts of Japan, for several years. Early in 1971, it was disclosed that many of the world's major oil companies had negotiated or were negotiating off-shore oil concessions with several of the governments of East Asia, including South Vietnam. Malcolm Caldwell argues in "Oil and the War—A Report from Singapore," *Liberation,* February-March-April 1971, that President Johnson must have been aware of the oil potential in the waters surrounding Thailand, Malaysia, Indonesia, and the Philippines when making his decision to go to war in Indochina, and he asks whether President Nixon has given the major oil companies a pledge to keep U. S. forces on the frontiers of East Asia. George W. Ball, the former under secretary of state, responds to such questions in "An Oil Spill in Troubled Waters," *Newsweek,* May 3, 1971, p. 51, by declaring that "in more than six years of involvement at the highest level of our government, I never heard even a whisper that America had a significant economic interest in Southeast Asia," a statement that will surely be recorded as a classic example of rhetorical overkill, if nothing else.

According to the *New York Times,* June 11, 1971, U. S. oil companies have exerted "considerable pressure" on the government of South Vietnam to prevent it from allowing the French to dominate the leasing of offshore oil rights. One American oil man said he told the Vietnamese minister of economy, Phan Kim Ngoc, that "if he let the French do this, then he could damn well ask the French for economic aid as well because the Americans wouldn't come through with it." The *Times* also reported that "it is believed that Deputy Ambassador Samuel D. Berger, at the urging of some American Oil representatives here, let it be known to Saigon that the United States would be perturbed if Mr. Ngoc favored the French."

policy generally? While a definitive answer is not possible, one does note with interest the large size of the Vietnam military market and the names of the firms who have taken the largest share of it: McDonnell Douglas, Lockheed, Grumman, Boeing, Ling Temco Vought, General Motors, General Electric, Standard Oil of New Jersey, Mobil Oil, U. S. Steel, Olin Mathiesson, Honeywell, and other aerospace and conglomerate giants.[4]

The kinds of decisions we would like to know more about are made at the upper reaches of government and in executive, that is, secret session. This is especially true in an age when wars are entered into by presidential fiat rather than through public debate and congressional declaration. Because of the inherently clandestine nature of executive decision-making, the public often learns what went on only when someone talks out of turn, when internal memoranda are leaked to the press, or upon publication of the memoirs of a participant. Still, it is safe to assume that the presidents, cabinet members, and other officials who were involved in the decisions to go to war in Vietnam and to escalate the war were aware that war means larger defense budgets, increases in military procurement, fat contracts, and high profits. To imagine that those in power divorce themselves from their corporate constituencies when deciding what to do with their power is naive and unrealistic.

Of course, no nation is commercially isolated. Vietnam is part of a region that stretches from the Indochina peninsula to Japan. It includes Malaysia, Indonesia, the Philippines, Taiwan, and Korea, and is dominated by mainland China. When one considers American business interests from this broader perspective, the economic factor emerges with greater force. Regardless of the size of U. S. commercial involvement in Vietnam, and it is considerable, the costs of the war, like any

4. See Council on Economic Priorities, *Economic Priorities Report,* February-March 1971, vol. 1, no. 7, for a listing and profiles of the largest war contractors.

other expression of our Asian foreign policy, should be evaluated in the context of U. S. interests in East Asia.

The nature of those interests can be understood in two ways: first, as in Vietnam, by considering the commercial fallout from U. S. military and military-related expenditures; second, by analyzing international trade patterns between the U. S. and East Asia.

Excluding the costs of the war in Vietnam and the costs of strategic nuclear weapons, total outlays for conventional forces in fiscal year 1970 were $44 billion. Of this amount, $19 billion went to Europe; over $16 billion went to Asia; and $1.3 billion to all other areas of the world.[5] Asia, in other words, creates the second greatest regional demand for U. S. non-war military expenditures. Obviously, with the costs of the war, Asia receives the largest American military investment by a wide margin.

Closely allied to U. S. military outlays in Asia are outlays for military assistance. Contrary to the government-fostered image of a relatively small and declining program, military grant assistance has been quite substantial and growing. It is also concentrated among the nations of East Asia. Official government sources have understated the size of this program by creating the impression that all outlays for it are embodied in the Military Assistance Program (MAP). It is true that MAP funds have gone down sharply in the past decade. Appropriations for MAP have declined from $1.8 billion in 1961 to $350 million in 1970. But a close examination of all federal expenditures for military assistance purposes reveals that MAP is now only a small slice of the military assistance pie.

Literally billions of dollars are spent for military aid to foreign countries outside of MAP, through such programs as support for "Free World Forces," the Food for Peace Program, subsidization of Vietnam piastres, and aid for counterinsur-

5. Charles Schultze, *Setting National Priorities* (Washington, D. C.: The Brookings Institution, 1970), p. 44.

gency and paramilitary activities. Total grant outlays amounted to approximately $4 billion in 1970 and, under the Nixon Doctrine, are scheduled to increase to about $6 billion in 1971 [6] and to go higher in future years. Although country-by-country breakdowns are considered classified information for some military aid programs, it is known that during the past several years, most of the dollars have gone to U. S. allies in East Asia, especially Vietnam, Thailand, Cambodia, and Korea. This trend is likely to continue.

In addition to the grant aid programs discussed so far, military sales are made to foreign countries through both government and commercial channels. Government sales have been averaging over a billion dollars per year. They dipped to $842 million in 1970, but are expected to exceed that amount in 1971. Commercial sales of military articles which, between 1965 and 1969, ranged between $274 million and $344 million, jumped to $567 million in 1970. Unlike the grant assistance program, military sales are made primarily with the industrialized nations. Most of this trade is carried on with Canada, the developed countries of Europe, and Israel. Still, the Department of Defense fact book on military assistance and foreign military sales shows that the East Asia and Pacific countries received deliveries of sales totaling $153 million in 1969.[7] According to the Pentagon: "The growing importance of foreign military sales (FMS) as an instrument of national policy is clearly apparent in light of the Nixon Doctrine. A key tenet of that doctrine is that in cases involving other types of aggression (i.e., non-nuclear) we shall furnish military and economic assistance when requested and as appropriate." [8]

The U. S. spent about $2.6 billion on economic assistance

6. These figures include the costs of navy ship loans and transfers of surplus and excess property which do not show up as budgetary outlays.
7. *Military Assistance and Foreign Military Sales Facts,* Department of Defense, March 1970, p. 24. East Asia and Pacific countries listed are Australia, Republic of China, Indochina, Indonesia, Japan, Korea, Malaysia, New Zealand, Philippines, Singapore, Thailand, and Vietnam.
8. Ibid., p. 19.

to foreign countries in 1970. About 25 percent of this amount went to East Asia. The aid consisted of shipments of food under the Food for Peace Program, funds administered by the Agency for International Development (AID), Export-Import Bank loans, and U. S. contributions to multilateral organizations such as the International Development Association which, in turn, loaned money to countries in this region.

Most importantly, foreign aid, in addition to whatever economic, political, and humanitarian objectives it serves abroad, is a prop to American business interests at home. As a matter of policy, at least 90 percent of all economic assistance funds are spent in the U. S., a point often made to promote foreign aid appropriations in Congress. The Industrial College of the Armed Services' manual on *Collective Defense and Foreign Assistance* states in response to the program's critics:

> The fact is that foreign assistance has been instrumental in maintaining the prosperity of several key segments of the American economy. In 1967 AID procured 96 percent of the commodities furnished under the foreign assistance program from American suppliers. This means that over $1.4 billion in commodities were purchased in the United States under the program in 1967, including $157 million in agricultural and industrial machinery, $150 million in chemicals, $127 million in motor vehicles, $120 million in iron and steel, and $109 million in fertilizers.[9]

Loans for economic development as well as grants are conditioned on U. S. purchases. Economic assistance is, in part, a subsidy to inefficient American industry.[10] (It seems hardly

9. Harold J. Clem, *Collective Defense and Foreign Assistance* (Washington, D. C., 1968), p. 26.
10. A similar point is made in Charles L. Schultze, Edward R. Fried, Alice M. Rivlin, and Nancy H. Teeters, *Setting National Priorities: The 1972* Budget (Washington, D. C.: The Brookings Institution, 1971), p. 130: "Development lending is now tied to procurement in the United States, which makes it a form of export promotion, particularly for some of our high-cost industries. The tying requirement, however, greatly reduces the value of these appropriations to the recipients, since they must pay prices higher than those on a competitive world market."

necessary to say that military spending and military assistance, too, operate as supports for inefficient American corporate enterprise.) Under the Nixon Doctrine, economic assistance is scheduled to increase, and more than likely East Asia's share will grow larger.

Asia is the United States's second largest trading partner outside of North America. We conduct somewhat larger trade with Western Europe, but our Asian trade has been catching up. For example, in 1955 exports to Western Europe totaled $5.1 billion, about double the $2.6 billion worth of goods exported to Asia. By 1970, exports to Western Europe had risen to $14.5 billion, nearly a three-fold increase, while exports to Asia had leaped to $10 billion, a four-fold increase. In 1970, imports from Asia reached $9.6 billion, exceeded only by imports from Western Europe and Canada. (Total U. S. exports in 1970 were $43.2 billion; imports were $40 billion.) Exports to Asia overtook exports to Canada for the first time in 1970. One can easily foresee the day when U. S. trade with Asia will be greater than with Western Europe. There are more people in Asia, more territory, and more potential wealth.

At least two important international trade considerations are not reflected in aggregate export-import statistics. One is the growing American dependency on foreign raw materials, machinery, transportation equipment, and iron and steel mill products. The other is the magnitude of U. S. investment abroad. While these phenomena are world-wide in scope, they do form a part of U. S. economic interests in Asia.[11]

(1) The U. S. has become, as Harry Magdoff has shown, a net importer of a wide variety of minerals and, in that sense, a resource-poor nation. Prior to World War II, the U. S. exported more minerals than it imported. Since that war, the situation has been reversed for several key minerals. Net imports as a percentage of total consumption have steadily grown. For ex-

11. For a detailed analysis see Harry Magdoff, *The Age of Imperialism: The Economics of U. S. Foreign Policy* (New York: Monthly Review Press, 1969), pp. 45–62.

ample, in 1968 (the latest year for which figures are available), we imported 35 percent of our iron ores and concentrates, 27 percent of our lead and zinc ores, 86 percent of our bauxite and other aluminum ores, 42 percent of our mercury ores and metallic mercury, and 95 percent of our manganese ores and concentrates. Although relatively small amounts of raw materials are imported from East Asia, large quantities of machinery, transportation equipment, and iron and steel mill products are purchased from this region, mostly from Japan. Further, the fact that the U. S. is a resource-poor nation with respect to minerals means that we will be constantly on the lookout for new sources of supply. The possibility that large oil reserves and perhaps other raw materials exist in East Asia is thus of more than passing interest.

(2) American manufacturing investments in foreign countries are a fair measure of the rise of the multinational corporation. In the past, this type of economic activity was not considered of great importance because the export of capital formed only a small percentage of total exports in any given year. It is now recognized that investments abroad have consequences that go far beyond the absolute dollars involved. Direct investments in foreign manufacturing are cumulative from year to year, unlike exports that are consumed, and produce enormous assets and productive capacities. As a result, the sales of U. S. foreign affiliates now exceed the value of U. S. exports. In 1969, U. S. direct investments abroad increased by $5.8 billion, bringing the book value of such assets to $70.8 billion. Sales of foreign manufacturing affiliates of U. S. firms amounted to $59.7 billion in 1968.[12] Moreover, the multinational corporation has enhanced the U. S. corporate sector's ability to influence the policies of foreign governments as well as its ability to penetrate foreign markets.

The net effect is to enlarge the stake that American business has in our own foreign policy, including our Asian for-

12. U. S. Department of Commerce, *Survey of Current Business,* October 1970, pp. 18, 26.

eign policy. Most direct investment abroad has so far been in Canada, Latin America, and Western Europe. But American firms have begun setting up affiliates and buying into companies in Japan, Australia, and the Philippines, and Singapore bristles with skyscrapers housing Far East headquarters of U. S. corporations. The book value of investments at the end of 1969 was $1.2 billion in Japan, $741 million in the Philippines, and over a billion dollars in other Asian and Pacific countries. Sales of U. S. manufacturing affiliates in Japan have soared from $380 million in 1961 to $2 billion in 1968; in the period 1966 through 1968 alone they doubled. In the Philippines, sales of affiliates have also risen sharply, from $160 million in 1961 to $410 million in 1968. Similar increases can be shown elsewhere in the Far East. Most assuredly, these trends will continue.

Japan, an industrial giant by any standard, is the keystone in the arch of U. S. economic relations with the Far East. With its population of over 100 million, greater than any West European nation, it is one of the United States's largest and most important business partners. The enlargement and exploitation of that business has long enticed American policy-makers, just as the possible loss of that business to mainland China and the communist nations has been enough to keep them in a state of high anxiety. Thus Eugene V. Rostow, former under secretary of state, has justified U. S. intervention in Vietnam on the basis of the long-range impact a withdrawal would have on Japanese policy, and on the fear "that the enormous masses and the geographical and strategic areas of that region will fall into the hands of hostile or potentially hostile powers." [13]

13. *The New Yorker*, July 4, 1970. One of the documents brought to light by the *New York Times*'s publication of *The Pentagon Papers* (New York: Bantam Books, Inc., 1971) is a 1952 National Security Council policy statement on "United States Objectives and Courses of Action With Respect to Southeast Asia." The statement holds that "The loss of any of the countries of Southeast Asia to communist aggression would have critical psychological, political and economic consequences." The region, defined in the document as Burma, Thailand, Indochina, Malaya, and Indonesia, is described as "the principal source of natural rubber and tin, and a producer of petroleum and

A similar view is implicit in the Nixon Doctrine. It is the policy of "containment" of China all over again. But China, with her growing trade and diplomatic relations with the West, is hardly contained. It is the United States, with its network of bases and its naval fleet in the Pacific, its logistical and budgetary nightmares, and its hydraheaded war in Indochina, that seems bottled up. Under the new foreign policy, it is possible that military costs in Asia will be reduced, more than likely in proportion to whatever downward pressures are maintained on the defense budget over the next several years. It is also possible that a more potent tactical nuclear force will be deployed in Asia, similar to the one that now exists in Europe, as U. S. manpower is drawn down.

Still, one might ask, why do we maintain all the old Asian commitments and practically all the bases, and why do we consider buttressing our "lower profile" with increased military aid and maybe tactical nuclear weapons? The answer, in my judgment, has a great deal to do with our economic involvement in Asia. Economics is not the sole determinant of foreign policy in Asia or any other region. But it would be a mistake to ignore or to relegate to low priority the economic factor in the name of structural or institutional imperatives. For one thing, political structure in a capitalist system is rooted in the allocation of wealth and resources. For another, a proper analysis of economic behavior must be conducted, in any case, from an institutionalist perspective. Our economic involvement in Asia is a more or less constant factor in the Asia equation and so long as it exists will exert significant influence on U. S. foreign policy.

other strategically important commodities. The rice exports of Burma and Thailand are critically important to Malaya, Ceylon, and Hong Kong and are of considerable significance to Japan and India. . . ." Moreover, "The loss of Southeast Asia, especially of Malaya and Indonesia, could result in such economic and political pressures in Japan as to make it extremely difficult to prevent Japan's eventual accommodation to communism." On June 18, 1971, the *Washington Post* published a 1954 policy statement of the National Security Council containing much of the same language of the 1952 document along with the following sentence: "Furthermore, this area was an important potential as a market for the industrialized countries of the free world."

The Economic Consequences of Intervention and Disengagement

SEYMOUR MELMAN: I will deal first with the economic consequences of disengagement.[1] The terms "intervention" and "disengagement" are not immediately clear in meaning. If a generalized interventionist policy continues, particularly in Vietnam, clearly something approximating the present number of divisions and types of equipment of the armed forces will prevail. However, even if there were a noninterventionist foreign policy, other military programs might continue and have predictable effects.

For example, a so-called heavy ABM system has been esti-

1. There is available a set of six volumes dealing with conversion of industry from a military to a civilian economy. The last of these, published recently by Praeger, completes a research program that began in 1961 and was conducted without foundation or governmental support by a graduate seminar in the Engineering School of Columbia University, which produced a considerable array of papers, the best of which are reproduced in these volumes. The Columbia papers are augmented by a study at Hofstra University by a colleague and friend, John Ullman, on the military electronics industry and its conversion prospects. There is a final volume by John Lynch, who is with the air force, on the problems of economic planning following military base closings. This last volume contains previously unavailable data, such as a twenty-page appendix table giving a complete listing of principal bases by state, together with data on numbers of civilian and military personnel on each base, capital investment, and payroll. Such data will be indispensable material for local economic planning, either by state or township. One of these volumes, called *The Defense Economy*, includes what is probably the best bibliography of these matters. The volumes are an efficient base from which further studies can be done, both on particular conversion planning and on collateral problems.

mated at approximately $50 billion. Given the record of final price versus initial estimate of major Defense Department systems—an average of 3.21—it might cost as much as $150 billion. Further, if the heavy ABM system were to afford protection for the populace under an airburst, such a feature would add approximately $500 billion for a population of 200 million. Here we lean on a rather good set of engineering cost calculations, done in 1962, which allowed for a modest factor of inflation of price and no allowance whatever for cost overruns. A system cost of $650 billion over five years would require an outlay of approximately $130 billion a year—almost doubling the budget of the federal government. These financial facts alone disclose consequences for the quantities of steel, concrete, skilled manpower, and the like that would be required. It would exhaust the supply of such material and manpower for other purposes, including other military purposes. Thus, the issue is not disengagement, but rather the entire nature of the military security policy of the United States, of which foreign engagement or intervention is but one facet.

An alternative policy to either three wars at once or two wars at once is required. One possible alternative military security policy for the United States could include three objectives. The first would be to operate a nuclear deterrent system. The second would be to maintain forces to guard the shores of the United States. The third would be to have forces to participate in international peace-keeping operations. Forces to perform these objectives in a technically first-rate fashion, together with backup in the ratio of approximately seven to one, could be about a million men, with budgets of one-third or less of the present budget. However tentative that sort of estimate, it does give an order of magnitude of the economic consequences of disengagement.

This conception of cost goes beyond disengagement from the Vietnam war. Furthermore, there might be disengagement from Vietnam; but there might still be a continuation of interventionist policy. The reports of the secretary of defense, in the period 1965 to 1967, identify possible locations of internal wars as candidates for intervention. This list includes Laos, Thailand, Burma, Indonesia, Iraq, Venezuela, Colombia, Bolivia, Guatemala, Uruguay, the Philippines, Nigeria, the Congo, Ghana, Uganda, and Burundi. Hence, the issue is not Vietnam or the Indochina war, but rather the whole policy of conducting military exercises of this sort.

Disengagement should be understood to mean turning off the policy of intervention. To know what that would imply, we have to examine certain principal parameters of the military-industrial system. In manpower terms, there are 2.9 million men in the uniformed armed forces. About three million are directly identified as working for the Department of Defense in industry and about one million are employees of the Department of Defense. Altogether, about seven million employees are directly involved. In addition, an assessment of those indirectly involved would extend to some portion of the employees of ball and roller bearing plants whose product is a military product but which are not traceably defined as operating for the Department of Defense. Also involved indirectly are the suppliers of civilian and other services to the persons who receive their primary income directly from the Department of Defense. In all, about eighteen million persons directly or indirectly derive their income from Defense Department expenditures. This constitutes 20 to 25 percent of the U. S. labor force of about 77 million. If one extends this number to include dependents, then clearly one is accounting for a substantial part of the population of the United States.

This economic activity is noteworthy for its geographic concentration. The recent reports of the Bureau of the Census, showing growth by states and counties, have special interest for this discussion. Areas of unusual population growth are highly correlated with areas of expansion of military industry and military base activity during the period of 1960 to 1970, precisely the period of major expansion of military organization and collateral activity. Budgets were enlarged under the

Kennedy and Johnson administrations from an order of $40 billion to $80 billion. Industrial concentration is chiefly in the aerospace, electronic, shipbuilding, and machinery industries, and in research and development. There is also occupational concentration in that these industries employ higher proportions of skilled personnel in their work force than do other industries. It is rarely the case anywhere else in the industrial system that 20 percent of the employees of a given establishment are technicians or engineers. Yet that is not uncommon in the aerospace, electronics, and related industries.

In considering the economic consequences of a major change of military security policy, it is critical to know the condition of preparation for coping with changeovers to civilian work. In 1964, Senator George McGovern initiated the first modern effort to establish a National Economic Conversion Commission. That early effort was viewed in less than friendly fashion by the Kennedy staffs; similarly by the new persons brought in by Lyndon Johnson. There was strong pressure to restrict the hearings on this bill, which enjoyed the co-sponsorship of some thirty members of the Senate, to a half-day of hearings in the Commerce Committee, devoted mainly to receipt and explication of letters from principal government departments, led off by the Department of Defense, all saying that such legislation was not needed.

I can supply some interesting background to the Department of Defense posture at that time. Before their statement was formally made, I arranged to meet with Enthoven and two of the other assistant secretaries. I argued that they should support the McGovern proposal on the grounds that if military industry developed capabilities for going civilian, then there was less incentive for it to stretch out its performance on military contracts in time or in cost. These men disagreed with my reasoning in this discussion. Thereafter, the Department of Defense appeared with a formal statement arguing that the McGovern bill was not needed and was undesirable.

In response to the McGovern and other senatorial initiatives, the Johnson administration countered by setting up what became known as the Ackley Committee, led by the chairman of the Council of Economic Advisors. This multi-agency committee deliberated and, after about a year, produced a report on the economic consequences of defense, recommending that an interagency committee would be sufficient to cope with all foreseeable problems of conversion, which they thought would fit within present fiscal and monetary policies. From time to time, from 1965 to 1970, persons concerned with these matters were told that the issue was in hand. However, as of December 1969, the Ackley Committee had not met for two years.

The next initiative on these matters was in 1969, again from Senator McGovern, and paralleled in the House. A fresh bill was prepared, which this time received co-sponsorship from about thirty-one members of the Senate. That bill was put in the hands of a subcommittee chaired by Senator Ribicoff, and has not been heard from since. Senator Ribicoff is from Connecticut, the state with the highest per capita income from military-industrial contract work. A more recent initiative on this matter occurred on December 1, 1969, in testimony presented by the late Walter Reuther, who proposed that it would be prudent to establish a federally controlled bank which would hold about 15 percent of profits before taxes from military contracts. These funds would be available to the management of the firms that had paid in the money, to be used by them for conversion and to insure the economic viability of their employees. This proposal would have provided a recoupment profit incentive to the management and stockholders of these firms.

Altogether, the present condition of preparation for a major change in military policy is near zero. The consequences are highly visible. The areas of concentration of the main military industries, including military research, are now unemployment disaster areas. Unemployment rates around Cambridge, Massachusetts, eastern Long Island, southern

New Jersey, Houston and Dallas, Los Angeles, San Francisco, and Seattle, are two to three times higher than the average for the country as a whole. The effects are most visible in the high technology occupations, those requiring technical degrees and long training. The response of the management of military-industrial firms to cutbacks of military contracts has simply been termination of the work force and termination of industrial activity. The prognosis of economics, relying on the classic wisdom of flexibility of resources and entrepreneurship, is plainly nonsensical.

These persons, with homes and personal and other investments in particular areas, find themselves in regions where the whole industrial system has gone into decline, and there are no prospects for them except through drastic change of job character or location. It would be in the interest of the country to establish a system for occupational conversion that would support former employees of the military industry at certain net income levels, depending on family size, of a minimal but decent sort for a period of two years. During that period, these men could reeducate themselves and go into fresh occupations. Many of these men face the prospect of having to learn a trade, since a considerable part of their skills are technically specific or unique to military products. It is notorious that cost minimization has not been a high priority factor in Defense Department industry management. Thus, we have engineers in great number who are magnificently competent to produce aircraft whose final price per pound approaches the price of gold, but are not competent to produce a commercial product like a tape recorder. It would also be appropriate to suspend mortgage payments, grant allowances for relocation, and provide medical insurance—to sustain the quality of life at a decent level and make it possible for men to retrain and apply their skills in productive work.

The experience of previous military industry and force cutbacks is germane to all of this. By 1944, the federal government decided that planning should be undertaken for the end of military operations, and at the instigation of Bernard Baruch, whose advice on these matters was taken seriously at the time, the federal government instituted a program of postwar planning. A committee for economic development was initiated to organize top industrial management in that direction, and every organization of any size had a vice president for postwar planning. A volume of articles appeared in technical journals and trade journals. There were conferences in industry, unions, technical societies, in the general press, and in economic literature, in addition to discussions among economists. The more critical material was in the form of detailed blueprinting of how to turn a factory or a firm around from military to civilian work.

In 1964, there was a moderate shift in military hardware requirements, and that experience occasioned the same sort of pattern that we see today. In 1970, there is a renewal of the 1964 pattern. However, it occurs in a situation where there has been a further accentuation of specialization in military work. This is bound to have the following consequences. The industries and plants involved will not be converted by their management except in most exceptional cases. I do not know of a single instance of a military products plant in the aerospace or electronics or shipbuilding or general machinery industries which has in the recent past been turned around to civilian work, or for which plans exist for a turnaround to civilian work. Managements do the easiest thing: cut losses and padlock the door. In many plants management has no jurisdiction with respect to conversion—in the Marietta plant of Lockheed Aircraft Company, for example, the structures and other useful objects are, in fact, government property. Managements of military industry firms and major laboratories have been asked from time to time to make proposals about what they might do, given a termination of their Defense Department work. Characteristically they have proposed that they continue doing work of a similar sort. They do not wish to be involved in any of the technology and engineering problems of the rest of society. Rather, they wish to operate essentially in a Defense Department-like environment, where they can service one customer and not have to cope with the problems of a changing institutional structure in a given industry or work force.[2]

There is a further constraint on the conversion of the work force. There are grounds for believing that an important part of the blue-collar work force in military industry has been spoiled for civilian work; that wage levels, habits of work, and workloads have taken on a quality in the military service firms such that their application to civilian products would ensure remarkably high costs or bankruptcy. Among engineers there is a particularly serious problem. These men do not orient themselves to minimizing costs. They do not understand the standardization of components or the design of circuits in modular fashion. They are prepared to install redundancy or unnecessary elaboration. The durability and reliability required for military products are hopelessly irrelevant to most civilian products. These technological orientations, which have been nourished by the Defense Department industrial machine, where costs are not counted, make these men unsuited for civilian employment. This is not to say that competence to do civilian work is not there or cannot be developed. It is to say that it is not automatically there, and that its development requires explicit planning and detailed and deliberate implementation.

The UAW (United Automobile Workers) proposal, delivered by Leonard Woodcock with the Reuther proposal, would

2. I have given substantial detail as to why this may be the case in the volume, *Pentagon Capitalism* (New York: McGraw-Hill, 1970). Further materials appear in the volumes of the Praeger series. Additional materials appear in periodicals on military industry management. You might also give serious attention to the remarks before Congress of Ernest Fitzgerald, who left the air force during the C-5A incident. He is an industrial engineer with very wide experience. He gave a detailed analysis of the characteristics of the military industry before my seminar at Columbia University in 1969. His diagnosis is consistent with materials gathered from other sources.

use the federal government to shore up the managements of military industry firms *after* they have attempted to undertake some civilian work. Such a procedure would probably mark a swift decline in the economic competence of a whole array of industries. If they could obtain this subsidization, they would also need subsidies in international markets. The rest of society would be paying dearly for this. To make possible an adaptation to a change of military security policy, a *prior* systematic formulation of industrial and occupational conversion is called for. First, industrial conversion must emphasize pressure on management to use detailed blueprinting for going civilian. Second, where particular managements are not interested or competent to do this—and this should be expected—their work forces must be backed up by a system similar to the GI Bill of Rights, for which any military industry ex-employee could apply and from which he could get reasonable support for himself and his family. The third requirement for the conversion process is the creation of new markets in all the areas of depletion in American society.

Next I want to sketch briefly the economic effects of a continuation of the present national security pattern, whether this is interpreted as a 2½ war or 1½ war doctrine or a Vietnam plus nuclear counterforce military security system.[3]

In July 1969, when the moon shot took place, President Nixon was describing as the greatest week since the Creation the very week in which New York City saw a concurrent failure of electricity supply, the telephone system, and the railroad system. The industrial infrastructure of New York City collapsed in the middle of 1969; and so, in the largest city in the United States, the characteristic condition of economic underdevelopment appeared.

The present power crisis is an extension of the same trend.

3. I have given a broad analysis of this sort in the volume, *Our Depleted Society* (New York: Holt, Rinehart, & Winston, Inc., 1965). The analysis is valid to this day without amendment; from 1965 to 1970, the data have proceeded in the same direction.

Generating capacity in electrical distribution systems is not constructible and installable except on a long lead time basis. Once designed, it takes more than a year to construct a large turbine or a large generator. To make any significant expansion in such equipment, it would be necessary to employ additional engineers in the electrical machinery industry and the electrical generating and distribution industry. But the major technical schools of the United States no longer give degrees in power engineering. They find it almost impossible even to hire professors in this field. Having lost about two generations of Ph.D.'s in this field, given an effort to enlarge the output of engineers trained in power, the United States would have to go to Sweden, England, Germany, even the USSR. Our engineering curricula have been set in the last decade to provide engineering suited for Department of Defense and NASA operations. Our electrical engineers for more than fifteen years have taken no courses in engineering economics. These men, even with the technical knowledge available, would not be competent to do the cost analysis for a simple tape recorder.

Depletion now exists in a number of our industries: machines, shipbuilding, steel, building. What is depletion? Depletion is the existence of an array of characteristics, including the following: zero research and development; zero employment of technically trained personnel; zero use of standardization and modular design; an unstable production system; organization of work on a job shop rather than production line basis. This condition prevails in a number of American industries and has rendered them incompetent not only to compete in foreign markets, but even to hold their own in domestic markets.

For example, machine tools is the industry of industries in a metal-using industrial system. Machine tools have the unique characteristics of being able to replicate themselves. When the machine tool stock in the manufacturing industries of the United States was counted in 1968, it was discovered that 64 percent of this equipment was ten years old or over, giving the United States the oldest stock of metal-working machinery of any major industrial country in the world—not necessarily the least efficient, but the oldest. This implies a dramatically slow rate of replacement of old equipment; hence, no offsetting of the rise in wages per hour by more efficient use of labor per hour; hence, rising unit labor costs; hence, rising prices. The same condition prevails in shipping and steel. In 1967, 17 percent of the U. S. domestic steel requirements were being met from abroad, and there is no foreseeable reversal of this trend.

Next, let us consider the export of industries. One of the little-appreciated features of the depletion process is that firms can often maintain financial competence by transferring the location of the work. In that way, the financial health of a company is retained but the productive competence of a society is diminished.

A whole series of services is in disrepair, of which health care is an outstanding case. The ratio of physicians in proportion to population in the United States has been declining since 1950—despite the importation into the United States of 2,500 to 3,000 physicians a year. In other words, the United States is robbing other countries of the output of twenty-five to thirty medical schools per year, to avoid the capital outlay and annual expense that would have to be sustained to produce them here. Present plans are for enlarging the number of medical schools by thirteen by 1975, not even enough to offset the importation of physicians, let alone the net domestic additional requirement for population growth.

Finally, let us look at the financial impact of the present military security policy and its continuation. To my knowledge, there is no text or monograph in economics that explains the occurrence of large-scale price inflation simultaneously with growing industrial unemployment. The reason is that our economists do not know, as a profession, how to differentiate between growth that is productive and growth that is parasitic. GNP, gross national product, means counting everything that is produced and sold. It is critical to understand that goods and services are productive only if they are useful as part of a level of living or for further production of some sort. In contrast to this, we produce a class of goods that is undesirable on these economic functional grounds. Military and related activity produces parasitic output. Upon being produced, it exits from the profitable exchange economy. A year ago, 8.3 percent of the gross national product consisted of this class of goods and services. There would not necessarily be inflationary pressure if there were, during the same period, an offsetting increase in the efficient output of goods and services. However, as against the 8.3 percent withdrawal, there was an increase in system output of only 1.9 percent. The difference between 8.3 and 1.9 is the pressure for an upward movement of prices.

Finally, depletion that is fed by priority allocation of manpower in a process of parasitic economic growth has a collateral effect of the most profound sort, both within and outside the United States. Inside the United States there are approximately 30 million persons who should be considered candidates for an economic development process. This population segment is characterized by high infant mortality, limited per capita income, and a high incidence of certain diseases. Economic development in the United States would cost approximately $50,000 per equivalent family unit. For 7.5 million equivalent family units, that is about $375 billion, or an annual outlay of $37 billion for ten years—about what the Vietnam war cost a year ago, and therefore not an inconceivable level of activity for a given project in our society. However, the present priority system for skilled manpower alone checkmates the possibility of this process in the United States.

The United States is similarly handicapped in participating, even given the will to do so, in economic development outside this country. Indeed, the main effect deriving from American domestic and international political and military priorities has been to suppress the economic development process elsewhere in the world through the process of accelerating military and related activity in many countries. A few years ago economists calculated the annual outlay for the developing countries of the world required to bring their rate of economic development to a level such that there was at least no longer a widening gap with the developed countries. What was needed was about an additional $18 billion a year. At that time, I mentioned this to well-placed persons in the American and Soviet governments, and both responded that it was preposterous to suppose that either or both of these governments would be able or willing to release resources of this magnitude. However, an examination of the data collated annually by the Arms Control and Disarmament Agency disclosed that $18 billion a year was the level of outlay of the underdeveloped countries of the world for their own military budgets. Thus the developing countries of the world have been burning up their total capital requirement for economic development in their military budgets, which, of course, are encouraged in all sorts of ways by the major powers.

This nation, and the Soviets as well, both for the same reasons, are in the grip of the process of depletion in many facets of their economies. Exit from this process of depletion is possible only as a consequence of a major change in military security policy and a major conversion of productive resources to truly economic use.

EARL C. RAVENAL: Your examination of our economic structure points to the failure of our policy-makers even to relate these serious disclosures to the continuation of our present posture in Asia. You also well illustrated the parasitical aspects of the relationship of the United States to the rest of the world. Also, I find it very constructive that you should interpret disengagement as a reduction essentially to a hemispheric defense posture and then trace its economic consequences. We ought to examine not only small adjustments in our posture, but major changes in our stance toward Asia and generally toward intervention—that is, containing violent change in the world. The inhibitions to the consideration of such alternatives in high policy-making circles would inspire an attitude of pessimism. You have pointed out structural impediments to reconversion and suggested the effect this might have on the choices of our political leaders regarding the defense budget and revision of our policy abroad. The net effect is a prohibition of rational consideration of major changes.

LEONARD RODBERG: I would like to put the comments that Seymour Melman made in a slightly different perspective, which makes the problem sound in one sense not as bad as he described it, but in another sense much worse. What he is talking about is less than one-third of the defense budget, that is, the $20 billion for procurement of major weapons using advanced technology. That $20 billion must be compared with two other numbers. One is the $70 to $80 billion of the total defense budget, which is the amount that would be affected by disengagement or by a substantial change in American foreign policy. The other number is $500 billion, which is roughly the total manufacturing output of the United States. Clearly defense production does not dominate American industry. However, the $70–80 billion defense budget is three-quarters of the controllable money that the Congress has available in the appropriation process, that is, the amount of money that it can put into one or another area of the American economy. The other $100 billion is fixed by prior statutes, trust funds, and so on. So the defense budget is eating up three-quarters of the tax dollars that we have available to deal with our social problems.

The real problem is that our present economic system cannot deal with the problems that industrial society is posing. This is not simply the fact that we put $20 billion in high technology areas of the defense complex. A private industrial economy simply can't cope with the social issues that are posed when you put millions of people together into an urban, neighborhood society. The whole economy is organized in the wrong way. In fact, looking at it in another way, the $70–80 billion defense budget is really the only way we have been able to maintain our economy for the past thirty years, and the fact that we have had to do that shows the failure of the present economic system to deal with the issues that face us.

SEYMOUR MELMAN: I find it enchanting to hear the latter comments. I have to be reminded from time to time that we really might have a private economy. My doubts come from observing that the state management system installed by McNamara in the Pentagon appropriates a larger bloc of capital funds than the total of industrial stock issues every year in this country. The private institution of Wall Street has simply been superseded by a government agency. Wall Street is left as a sort of backwater clerical service for transactions and the like.

Economists have said that if the GNP is going up and there is full employment, then everything is fine. But you must differentiate: Full employment for what? A growing GNP of what composition? In a number of European cities, for example London, the air is actually getting better. Rivers are becoming clearer. Splendid transportation systems operate in a number of places, notably Hamburg. Now the economy of Germany is about as "private" as the American economy. So I suspect that we should turn our attention away from traditional categories like "private," and pay more attention to a system of control that combines private ownership with quite a lot of public control. At times, control is invested in groups of private entities. The private industries of Japan group themselves together in a way that comes out looking very much like national planning.

THOMAS A. DINE (legislative assistant to Senator Church): There is a proposal by Senator Kennedy dealing with the conversion of industries which have been primarily involved in military operations. I wonder if you might comment on this proposal.

SEYMOUR MELMAN: I think the Kennedy proposal is tailor-made to keep intact some of the big military research and development shops, like the ones in his home state. This would not be in the interest of the United States, because these institutions, as *institutions,* are probably not convertible. Only the individuals are. The reason is this: the managers of these institutions and the institutional capabilities are oriented to Defense Department and NASA problems. In one case that I know, a civilian-activity division of a research and development institution is prevented from expanding because corporate management is overwhelmingly made up of men who made their mark working in and around the Defense Department and do not wish to be superseded by people with civilian-industry capability and orientation. So in order to retain their decision-making power, the Defense Department-oriented men have prevented further development in civilian directions. Now activity of that sort is to be expected all over. For these reasons, conversion of institutions, no. Conversion of people, yes. Hence, my emphasis on occupational conversion.

MARCUS G. RASKIN: I am concerned in Seymour Melman's analysis about the phrase that he used: that we should go out and get new markets. Some people do not accept this analysis and think that new markets are another form of internal-external imperialism that implies the making of things which shouldn't be made at all, the overriding of other people's cultures, and the perpetuation of a system which has generated the national security state structure in the first place.

SEYMOUR MELMAN: By markets I mean something quite different. For example, one of the things that is in desperate need today is housing, especially in and around cities. But needs are not the same thing as markets. To create a real market, considerable funds must be allocated with the stipulation that there be institutions to deliver according to specifications, within a stated cost, and over a stated period of time. That would induce energetic persons to devise the technical means and organization, and there would be something that a lot of serious people would bid for. It would be good for them. They would have a lot of reasonably compensated work to do. And it would be splendid for society. That is what I mean by new markets.

Now suppose you say that it makes a difference who controls this building activity; that this will affect the configuration of its use and the relation of houses to other facilities. I would agree that there are many options: unplanned or planned use? planned by whom? and with what degree of popular involvement? There are major political and social choices there, and those choices do mean something. But we are still at a primitive level with respect to this problem. We are still at the stage of providing floor space. Only after there has been a tangible undertaking will it be appropriate to get engrossed in problems of configuration of design and methods of control.

V

APPROACHES TO CHINA:

ACCOMMODATION OR CONTAINMENT?

The One China
and the Two Chinas

EARL C. RAVENAL: It is no secret that this country's China policy has been under intensive review by the Nixon administration. Also, it takes no great speculative gift to predict that our perennial attempt to deny the admission of mainland China to the United Nations will inevitably be rebuked by the majority of the U. N. membership.[1] So this might be a worthy occasion to review some of the indications of a changing attitude and consideration on the part of our government that might lead to certain initiatives as we approach the 1971 U. N. session.

A certain spirit of enlightenment seems to have reappeared among State Department and other government officials concerned with this problem. To a discernible extent, the cramped and unimaginative dogmatism that characterized official pronouncements on China seems to be lifting. At least the cautious but relatively objective and balanced observations and advice of the orthodox sinologists are being received and are having an effect. Whether history has already outrun this cautious advice, and the times loudly call even for a much more realistic and un-self-serving approach than this, is an

1. The General Assembly of the United Nations voted 51 to 49, on November 20, 1970, for the Albanian resolution to seat Peking and expel Taipei. The proposal was, however, characterized as an "important question" that required two-thirds support.

open question and perhaps the critical question of this conference.

During 1970, communist China has pragmatically sought to overcome some of the setbacks it incurred during the four-year Cultural Revolution. Indeed, it appears that the People's Republic of China preserved its inherent strengths to a greater extent than generally credited. It has emerged with its agricultural system and basic living standards in rather good shape. Fortunately for the Chinese, they have experienced a decade of good agricultural crops. Foreign trade is almost at the levels of before the Cultural Revolution: close to $4 billion for the year 1969.

However, even after the purging of the former chief of state, Liu Shao Chi, and of a vast portion of the military and civil bureaucracies, the leadership is not yet fully cohesive again, and there is some evidence of remaining differences in domestic—particularly economic—policy. There has not yet been a fourth Five Year Plan, and the 1970 economic plan was only belatedly approved. There is still a jockeying for position as party and government structures are rebuilt.

As for their security interests, the Chinese are not only concerned about their northern borders, but of course they continue to be concerned in the south. They will continue, as a matter of basic policy, to seek a buffer to the south, and will attempt to bring about a withdrawal of the U. S. presence. They also have a growing concern about the emergence of Japan. Whereas there has been a triangular power relationship in Asia and the Pacific for some time, Japan has virtually already made it a quadrangular relationship.

In recent months, Peking has initiated a remarkable diplomatic offensive. It has dispatched twenty-eight ambassadors abroad, as compared to the one ambassador it retained during the major part of the Cultural Revolution. That leaves some sixteen missions still headed by chargés d'affaires. In addition, it has expressed an interest in gaining a seat in the United Nations, after precluding that possibility for many years by insisting on certain prerequisites which were unacceptable to most members. Now only one condition remains: the ouster of the government of the Republic of China.

As for our bilateral relations with China, the United States, though still unwavering in its expressed commitment to Taiwan, has taken certain unilateral steps. In July 1969, we allowed tourist purchases of up to a hundred dollars of Chinese goods. At the same time, we relaxed restrictions on travel to mainland China on an American passport. Over nine hundred passports have been validated for travel to communist China, but from the beginning of the Cultural Revolution until September 1970, the Chinese have admitted only three Americans on validated passports.[2] In December 1969 we allowed unlimited noncommerical purchases, removing the hundred-dollar restriction. In the same month we permitted American-controlled foreign subsidiaries to conduct nonstrategic trade with mainland China. In April 1970 we allowed selective shipments of American-made components and related spare parts for nonstrategic foreign goods to be exported to China. In August 1970 we lifted restrictions on American oil companies abroad selling oil to noncommunist ships bearing nonstrategic cargo to Chinese ports. In late 1969 we virtually eliminated the Taiwan Straits patrol. Also, the Chinese have met with us twice this year at Warsaw. A third scheduled meeting was canceled because of Cambodia.

Some other steps are under consideration, which include totally lifting travel restrictions, totally lifting nonstrategic trade restrictions, in general treating China on a level with the Soviet Union,[3] and even pulling out military forces from Taiwan as the Vietnam war winds down (this move would be possible

2. During the "Ping-Pong" initiatives of April 1971, China welcomed the U. S. table tennis team and several newsmen. In March 1971 the U. S. had removed restrictions on passports for travel to the People's Republic of China.
3. On April 14, 1971, President Nixon announced the lifting of the twenty-one-year-old ban on direct trade with China in nonstrategic goods. The list of excluded strategic items was decided on June 10, 1971. Nixon also permitted U. S. vessels and aircraft to carry Chinese cargo between non-Chinese ports and allowed U. S.-owned but foreign-registered vessels to call at Chinese ports. Other concurrent moves expedited Chinese visitors to the U. S. and relaxed certain currency controls.

on purely technical grounds). Dual representation in the United Nations has been suggested unofficially within the Nixon administration.[4] Avoidance of provocative actions in the vicinity of the mainland,[5] rejection of development of an anti-Chinese ABM, and broadening or even upgrading of the Warsaw talks are other suggestions that have been considered.[6]

With respect to such moves, two general courses are available. The first would be to take action unilaterally, without the expectation of a Peking response—since many of the remaining restrictions and postures are relics of the Korean War. The second is to wait for a more tangible response by Peking before taking further steps. The Chinese themselves, of course, have returned to the status quo of before the Korean War and might expect us to do the same without additional reciprocation on their part. Also, however, they do not especially require travel between the two countries at this point, nor do they particularly need to trade with us, since they are already obtaining the goods they could get from us. Some of our allies, such as Japan, the U. K., West Germany, France, Canada, and Australia, are enjoying and profiting from the absence of U. S. competition in their growing trade with mainland China, which is trading considerably more with the noncommunist countries than with other communist countries. (Only $785 million of a total of $3.9 billion in 1969 was with other communist countries.)

So the U. S. posture has already changed, in certain modest but tangible ways, but we have not brought overall policy into line with it. The most serious obstacle to any effort to reach an accommodation with the People's Republic of China is the problem of Taiwan, which remains under the control of a

4. Secretary of State Rogers, on August 2, 1971, officially announced a Two China policy in relation to the U. N.
5. The U. S. has suspended reconaissance overflights of the mainland and intelligence patrols into Southern China.
6. From July 9 to July 11, 1971, Henry Kissinger, President Nixon's assistant for national security affairs, talked with Premier Chou En-lai in Peking and arranged for a presidential visit to China, to take place before May 1972.

government which challenges the legitimacy of the People's Republic of China. The U. S. commitment to the defense of Taiwan and the Pescadores, the continuing of diplomatic recognition, and the support which we have given it internationally, have been the primary obstacles to improving relations with mainland China.

Of course, despite the fact that the form of our policy toward the Republic of China has remained unchanged for twenty years, there has been some change in the substance of that policy, and some recognition of a change in the interests that underlie the policy. Originally, in the broad context of isolation and containment, this policy assigned a very special strategic importance to Taiwan. It supported the government of the Republic of China as an alternative to what in those days was described as "the Chinese communist experiment" on the mainland. In pursuit of these interests the U. S. extended to the Republic of China very substantial military and economic assistance, and defended its international position as the only legitimate government of China. In the mid-1960s, because militarily the likelihood of a Chinese communist attack was perceived to have receded, Taiwan became less important to the U. S. It remains primarily as a logistic base in support of operations in Vietnam, rather than as a listening post.

More important, apparently, in terms of the perceptions of U. S. policy-makers, as they relate to Taiwan, has been the fact that, with the substantial economic assistance we provided, Taiwan achieved high economic growth and structural change, that continued even after the termination of our economic aid in 1965. Internationally, Taiwan under the government of the Republic of China has been active in assisting other countries in advancing their own economic development. This activity has enhanced the position of the Republic of China with many of the countries of East Asia, both as a trading partner and as a participant in regional efforts. An example is her relationship with Japan. In 1966 it was hard to raise any interest among most Japanese, official or unofficial, on the question of Taiwan. That is not true today. In the Nixon-Sato communiqué of 1969, and more particularly in Sato's address before the National Press Club, Taiwan was included among the national security interests of Japan; certainly the Japanese economic interest there is very large now, both in trade and investment.

Both Peking and Taipei consider that the civil war continues. The government of the Republic of China on Taiwan refuses to accept any compromise, domestically or internationally, of its claim to be the government of China, and both Peking and Taipei insist that Taiwan is part of China. The People's Republic of China insists that there can be no fundamental change in U. S.-PRC governmental relations until the United States ends its military presence on Taiwan; and it claims further that it has the right to resolve the problem of Taiwan, which it considers an internal matter, by whatever means are necessary, including the use of force.

The position now expressed by officials of the U. S. State Department is that (1) the dispute between the government of mainland China and the government on Taiwan, as well as the status of Taiwan itself in its relationship to the mainland, are matters to be resolved by the parties directly concerned, not matters to be negotiated between the United States and one of those parties; (2) as long as this is achieved by peaceful means, no vital U. S. interest is likely to be seriously affected; (3) until such a resolution is achieved, the U. S. is prepared to deal with both governments as competent authorities over the territory they now control; and (4) with respect to the Republic of China, the U. S. will maintain its defense commitment and support for the government on Taiwan as a member of the international community.

Since there is little prospect in the foreseeable future of a peaceful resolution of this dispute between Peking and Taiwan, or of the status of Taiwan, the inflexibility of the government of the Republic of China, both in terms of the political structure on Taiwan and the defense of its international position, could still create serious problems for the United States. We may have difficulty in retaining international support for the Republic of China on any basis in the face of the insistence of the People's Republic of China that Taiwan is part of China. These difficulties are likely to come about as a result of an erosion in the Republic of China's bilateral relations. Canada and Italy both are prepared to sever diplomatic relations with the Republic of China if they can reach an agreement with Peking.[7] Further, the U. S. government recognizes that loss of membership in the United Nations for the government of the Republic of China could create serious problems in maintaining international standing for Taiwan and its present government. It also recognizes that the domestic political situation in Taiwan is inherently unstable by virtue of the fact that the majority of the Taiwanese population, the approximately twelve million people who are Taiwanese, who were there before the government of the Republic of China came from the mainland, have no real voice in the central government's policies. There are factors or possibilities which could lead to an explosion: the death of Chiang Kai-shek, a major foreign policy setback, or an economic crisis.

There is also the problem that the Republic of China continues to maintain a disproportionately large military establishment; and the cost of that establishment is heavy—about 10 percent of its GNP and over 50 percent of its budget. If it had to cover all its military expenditures, there might well be a serious setback to the present economic growth rates. So the U. S. has felt itself pressed to extend massive military assistance over the past fifteen years, to enable the Republic of China to carry a military establishment vastly in excess of its defense needs without prejudicing its economy. Efforts have been made by the U. S. government to get it to reduce the size

7. Both these countries recognized the Peking government in November 1970 and "took note" of Peking's political claim to Taiwan. The Taipei government promptly severed diplomatic relations with both countries.

of its defense establishment. But the Republic of China looks at the size of its defense establishment not as something to be determined simply by calculation of defense requirements, but as a symbol of the return to the mainland.

So Taiwan, in several dimensions, will be the principal obstacle—or the major challenge—to the creation of a constructive and stable relationship between the U. S. and the People's Republic of China.

The Chinese Threat and
the Problem of Deterrence

WILLIAM W. WHITSON: I want to address three broad topics: first, the alternative meanings of "the Chinese threat" and the problem of defining it within the larger context of Asian international relations; second, domestic Chinese constraints on their military policies, particularly on their ability to project military power beyond their borders; third, the major problems and opportunities confronting American planners and our allies in designing policies, force structures, base postures, and so forth. These policies, insofar as they seek to deter Chinese aggression, should be designed to reinforce Chinese domestic *constraints*.

Much time and energy have been spent over the last few years on military threat analysis. The normal approach to threat analysis involves a search for an active quantifiable constraint on an adversary's ability to project military power —usually a geographic constraint, and industrial constraint, or a logistical constraint. As a consequence of this kind of focus, "military threat" has come to be defined largely in terms of a specific level of manpower and firepower supportable over a particular period of time at specific distances from the adversary. In the case of China, this has been translated into a "worst case," that is, a maximum number of Chinese divisions that could operate across the southern border or the Korean border.

The focal question that I pose, in defining the Chinese threat, is: is such worst-case military threat analysis the best basis for designing our own and allied force postures and base structures? The summary answer is no. In order to underscore why I feel that this is the wrong approach, I will dwell briefly on the budget process. In searching for force levels and budgetary resources, you can start either with the budget constraint or the enemy threat side and work your way to an appropriate strategy for coping with only those threats that match budget ceilings. I am speaking of political and economic, as well as military, strategies. Strategists would prefer to start the analytical process by first identifying alternative threats and then strategies. Once you have a strategy or alternative strategies, you can discuss missions. Eventually you arrive at the resources necessary to support the missions. And there you can split resources between United States and allies. On the other hand, politicians and practical policy-makers prefer to start the analytical process by first estimating alternative budget ceilings.

A key word in either case is "alternatives." There is no such thing as a single fixed U. S. interest or a single strategy or a single threat. These are all judgmental. However, some focus to "interests" may emerge if you can define American interests in terms of several dimensions toward a particular country, including: (1) the general rationale for what we hope to achieve in our relationship with that country over the next decade; (2) the diplomatic elaboration, that is, the propaganda or verbal elaboration of that rationale; (3) U. S. military assistance and the host country military component; (4) U. S. economic assistance; (5) the nuclear weapons component; (6) the attitude the United States might take toward domestic politics in that country, that is, the extent to which we would involve ourselves in that country's domestic politics or worry about whether democracy exists in that country—whether that should or should not be a determinant of what we give or do;

and (7) the relationship between the host country and third countries.

Suppose you took these factors to define the relationship we would like to achieve. It is evident that these are not fixed, that they can easily shift over a decade. Take the example of Korea, where in late 1949 or early 1950 we had reasonably well established through a long process of analysis how we would respond in the event of invasion. You could have said that we had reached relatively clearly thought-out priorities. Yet suddenly, when the invasion came, overnight a few men turned this around. It is illusory to say that interests are objective, fixed, long-term, and something that can be relied upon —that is a first major source of ambiguity. Yet you cannot talk about a threat in the abstract—you must talk about a threat to some U. S. and allied interest, usually a perceived, short-term interest.

Given the ambiguity between short- and long-term interests, military planners have tended to focus on the "purely military aspects" of both the threat and the response. Yet they have discovered that our ability to predict military capabilities through war-gaming techniques or through case studies is very limited. It used to be that one could assume that big battalions, firepower, and manpower could determine the outcome of battle. But among the other lessons of Vietnam, it is clear that if you focus only on those "quantifiables," you are going to miss the outcome by a long way. There are many other important components involved. In addition to ambiguities arising from the state of the art of the security policy process as well as its military component, we must evaluate perceptions on the part of Asian countries—not just the American model of what the threat looks like, but the perception of a Burmese, a Cambodian, a Laotian government of the Chinese or any other threat, not only external but internal. Therefore, it may be more fruitful, instead of talking about particular force levels and whether or not the Chinese could sustain such force levels in moving across the border, to discuss the question of constraints on any Chinese projection of military power, regardless of the amount.

I will deal with four political trends and extrapolate their effects into the 1970s in the political, economic, and military spheres in China. The first trend in China is an ongoing struggle for both national and regional power between central and regional groups. This trend is not going to stop; it has been going on for many years, since long before the communists took power in Peking. It has been exacerbated by the Cultural Revolution, and you can expect this trend to continue. China, like any other country, is a political system, not a monolith with one man at the top handing down rules and everybody marching shoulder to shoulder.

The second trend concerns the focus of power which has shifted away from the center toward regional authority. This was dramatized during the Cultural Revolution. A good deal of debate still goes on about where power lies in China, but the destruction of the Party, leaving the military as the only truly national organization with its power and its formal and informal lines of communications largely intact in local areas, has reinforced a trend toward regionalism.

The third trend has been the development in the past—and one that will continue in the future—of the power of three military regions in China: the Shenyang military region in Manchuria, the Nanking military region along the east coast, and the Canton military region. The majority of Chinese industrial power, population, and military power is concentrated in those three regions. And the three regional commanders—with the exception of Huang Yung-sheng who was the regional commander of Canton and now is the Chief of General Staff—are the only regional-level military commanders now in the Politburo. I believe this symbolizes their primacy over the other twelve military regions.

A fourth political trend in China, that incorporates or summarizes the others, is the likelihood that China will continue as a coalition regime. In other words, we are not really accurate when we talk about Peking or China as a Maoist regime. Instead, what seems to have happened in China is that a coalition either of military regional commanders or regional political and civil figures now are engaged in a dialogue between Peking and the regions and provinces about resource allocations, both for internal and external purposes. Personally, I am not convinced that Peking has ever been the Maoist personal dictatorship that Chinese propaganda might have led us to believe. Instead, emerging evidence and well-established political theory suggest that this political dialogue, a constant bargaining process for power, status, and resource allocations, has been going on for twenty years at least.

Now shifting to the economic sphere, there are three trends that are worth noting. The first is that, as in the 1960s, so in the 1970s the central leadership will probably have great difficulty in taxing the surplus wealth of the regions, particularly the wealthier regions of China. It appears that the first economic decentralization was started in 1956, faltered, and has again been revived. Recently, there has been a revival of many small light consumer-goods factories. In part the rationale for this trend is war preparedness, dispersal for national defense. But perhaps more important for the central regime in trying to mobilize excess resources and import foreign technology has been its difficulty in taxing interregional grain transfers. In fact, local authority appears to have been very reluctant to transfer surplus grain either to other regions or to central use.

There is a second military and economic trend that is a counterpoint in opposition to the first. That is the apparent power of the central military elite to control heavy arms industry, ranging from advanced weapons programs to tanks and aircraft. It appears, from our knowledge of the distribution of military industry around China, that there has been a deliberate effort to prevent any single military regional commander from having a monopoly over a major weapon. The components of these various major assemblies seem to be distributed in such a way that while there might be final assembly in one region, yet a military regional commander, if he had any illusions about warlordism, would have difficulty in doing this without the help of some other regional commander.

The third economic trend has to do with China's ability to project her military power beyond her borders through the expansion of her arms industry. It is very unlikely that the heavy arms industry in China will expand very rapidly during the 1970s. Again this is because of the factors of local control of resources and the perceptions of the senior military people of their limitations. These factors will constrain their willingness to sacrifice great resources for heavy arms production, partly because they do not feel they need them.

As for military trends, perhaps the most significant military trend in the 1970s will be a continued primacy of military figures in the total national polity. We know that the People's Liberation Army remained the only national institution that really survived the Cultural Revolution, from the military special administrative committees up to the central government. But more than that, if you look at percentage figures on the Ninth Central Committee, which was elected in April 1969, some 65 percent of the full number of members of the committee are military figures. The military is obviously having a great influence over the rebuilding of the party from the ground up. Their past behavior suggests that the professional military men in China are a little disdainful of the promises of political ideologues, of slogans with fast remedies for the many problems that confront China. They have joined the club of Asian military people who, initially for reformist reasons, took over their own governments.

A second military trend has to do with their perceptions of geographic priorities. From their forty years of working with and fighting with each other, Chinese military leaders have learned that the greatest threats are internal—that is, the greatest threats to their own political status. In part this is another manifestation of the Middle Kingdom syndrome: that the thing that really counts in this world is what happens in China. Certainly for the purpose of promotion, status, and political future, this has been the case in the past.

A third military trend concerns the pace of military modernization. It is likely to be slow, because the majority of the regional commanders and the local figures, and in fact the majority of the people in the high command in Peking, have had very limited experience with sophisticated weapons. They have had a very shallow record of joint operations and joint maneuvers. If in fact an internal threat is more important in their perspective and their calculus of needs, particularly the threat of a peasant uprising—of which there have been quite a number over the last fifteen years, though not of the degree or type of a rebellion—that specter is something that must always be a sort of baseline concern for Chinese political and military leaders. The kinds of weapons they need for local control really don't have to be nuclear weapons or very sophisticated weapons. This is not to say that there is not going to be an argument about this. The Chinese communist military leaders are coming to a period in their military bureaucratic history which is comparable to the period from 1935 to 1955 in American military bureaucratic history; that is, the interservice rivalry period is upon them. As nuclear weapons come on stage, who gets to control them, who gets the budgetary resources, who gets the political status and power that go with those resources—these problems are going to confront the Chinese air force commanders versus naval and ground force commanders. This contention will probably be a central one.

A fourth military trend is their emphasis on defense. There has been a tendency to accept the notion that China is competing for global power status and is fully committed to an early attainment of a great power status comparable to the United States and the USSR. While this may be true in political terms, if you analyze the structure of their military resources, those resources and their distribution suggest that China is concerned first with internal and next, at most, with Asian regional adversaries, and that the concern for global adversaries —projecting their power to Africa or to the deep ocean—is simply not reflected in their design of their military weapons systems.

A fifth military trend is the design and employment of nuclear weapons. Here, instead of seeing a massive attention to ICBMs, we are probably going to see an emphasis on medium-range missiles. They are also slowly building medium-range bombers. Therefore, we can expect them to focus on delivery systems which will accent the immediate Asian perimeter and the adversaries they see there, both nuclear and nonnuclear.

A sixth military trend has to do with the Chinese ability to concentrate and mobilize military resources in the event of a threat. Because of the political and economic constraints and the regionalism that is reflected in the distribution and mobility of Chinese military resources since the Korean War, their resources are in fact very immobile. They have been tied down not only for political reasons, but probably because of an agreed strategic plan for the defense of China in separate military regions. That is, instead of defending China in the event of an invasion by a series of lines or fall-back positions similar to those that were used by Chiang Kai-shek in the Sino-Japanese War, or instead of concentrating military resources and throwing those resources to a threatened point as we might do if we were confronted by a direct invasion, the Chinese seem to have deployed their resources in such a way as to permit each military region to defend only *itself* in the event of an invasion, with the center having available to it certain resources such as tactical air, navy, engineers, missile artillery, research and development, which the center can use as levers over, and as reinforcements in support of, the regions.

These trends reflect and promise three alternate strategies

that are available to the Chinese. All of these strategies are essentially defensive. First, in Northeast Asia they would appear to have a hostage strategy. Since they cannot reach the United States directly with retaliatory power, at least they can prove that they could badly damage a major American client, that is, the Japanese or the Koreans. They can convey the same kind of political message to the Russians. With their medium-range missiles along the east coast and in northeast China, they can persuasively follow the same strategy the Russians employed toward the United States in the 1940s and early 1950s, when they also had no intercontinental ballistic missiles, but could badly damage Western Europe if the United States launched a first strike. Second, in Southeast Asia the Chinese are likely to follow what is best characterized as a buffer strategy: to create a buffer zone where the distribution of power along the southern borders would remain rather ambiguous. The military resource requirements for this kind of strategy can be relatively small: several Chinese divisions near the border and a small input of weapons and advisers for insurgency operations. Finally, if those two major deterrent strategies should fail, if an invader should attack the China mainland, their continental defense strategy would seem to call for a decentralized defense that I described earlier.

There are a great many foreign constraints that have been working on the Chinese. One set of constraints comes from the Soviet Union, particularly the Soviet military buildup on the northern border. Another constraint has been the American buildup of air power and sea power in East and Southeast Asia. China is surrounded by adversaries. It is curious, though, that in response to clearly perceived threats (other than the Korean War)—that is, the two Taiwan Straits crises, the Soviet threat from 1966 onward, or even the Vietnam war —the Chinese did not allocate massive military resources. Conversely, during the Cultural Revolution, when internal political problems confronted the Chinese, relatively dramatic movements took place, with fairly large units. This suggests that the Chinese are much more concerned with and much more constrained by internal political developments than by political or military signals that either the Russians or the United States might think they are sending to the Chinese from the outside.

If we assume that there are so many domestic constraints working against Chinese projection of significant military power, what events might upset this and turn this general trend line around? At least five events would have to be listed —probably a much longer list—and three of them would be foreign events. First, if they perceived an imminent ground invasion of China, then you might see some significant shifts of resources internally.

Second, if they perceived the probability of the physical occupation and political control of key areas contiguous to China—not necessarily areas which the Chinese wish to occupy but areas which they look upon as we look upon a Russian missile installation in Cuba—as buffer areas whose occupation by a foreign power would be too threatening, there could be a major redistribution of forces.

Third, the threat of a foreign air attack: if it looked as if the distribution of air power were such as to threaten this, either unilaterally on the part of the Americans or bilaterally with Americans and Russians—if in a coincidental way the Chinese saw a deployment of air power as portending an attack, especially on their nuclear facilities—then you would probably see some major movements of Chinese military power, especially within their air defense system.

The last two kinds of events are internal. Fourth, if there were a major peasant uprising, either in sympathy with what might be perceived as an external threat or for internal reasons, you could expect the fairly self-centered, self-serving military regional commanders to sacrifice some of their resources to cope with this, even in another region.

Finally, if there were the threat of military dictatorship in China, in the sense that Maoists and party administrators and

economic planners were completely dominated by military figures, then I think you might see a major political as well as
military reallocation of resources.

The problem for American deterrent force planners is, instead of accenting weapons which will deter Chinese nuclear
power from striking against the United States or which will
deter Chinese conventional force deployments to Southeast
Asia or elsewhere, rather to design force postures in such a
way as to reinforce those domestic constraints that already
exist in China. The true deterrent effect of such measures
would be far greater than the *provocative* effects of alternative
American and allied force postures—including some aspects
of the current allied force distribution in Asia—which do not
work to reinforce Chinese domestic constraints.

Ending the Permanent
Confrontation with China

FRANZ SCHURMAN: I offer my remarks not as a critic of American foreign policy, but as an opponent of that policy.

Since the end of World War II and the beginning of the cold war, there has not been a single unified American foreign policy. In fact, there have been a number of policies which mirrored the power conflicts and struggles within the government, struggles which should be far more publicized than they have been.

I see three basic currents since the end of World War II which have been determinants of American foreign policy: anticommunism, containment, and peaceful coexistence. Anticommunism is essentially an ideological outlook which sees the world as divided into two forces, with permanent war between them which has to lead to victory for one or the other side. The practical American response associated with anticommunism is rollback.

Containment has been understood to mean stopping the expansion of the great communist powers, Russia and China. But the success criterion of containment, as originally evolved in Europe, was the creation of blocs of nations—economic, political, and military alliances to form a barrier against communist nations. Dean Rusk's policy in Southeast Asia was containment. The essential element in containment has been the drawing of demarcation lines.

Peaceful coexistence has a strong economic basis. That current grew out of Henry Morgenthau's grandiose plans for the post-World War II world—that world unity will be brought about by trade. For all its apparent benignness, peaceful coexistence is the most imperialistic of the currents, envisaging a truly global role for America.

Around the late 1950s, major changes took place in the interaction of these three currents as they determined concrete American foreign policy. In addition to anticommunism and containment, the U. S. began stressing peaceful coexistence. But whereas the U. S. adopted a mix of containment and peaceful coexistence toward Russia, it opted for a mix of containment and anticommunism toward China. Paraphrasing Kennedy, the Chinese said: the olive branch for the Russians and the sword for us.

While anticommunism in East Asia took the overt form of counterinsurgency, at the same time rollback too was practiced. From bases in Laos and Taiwan, the U. S. did everything it could to harass China. As the air war now rages in Indochina, it still is impossible to say this is just a containment-oriented counterinsurgency. Anticommunists in the American government and military still dream of rollback.

Containment took the form of trying to duplicate what was achieved in Europe. Rusk and McNamara tried hard to get Asian nations to send troops to Vietnam. Numerous attempts were made by the U. S. to launch political and economic cooperation. The U. S. tried to bring Japan into the picture, not as an equal partner but as a strong and powerful servant of the U. S. Both containment and anticommunism have failed. The Nixon Doctrine marks the transition from that failure to something else not yet clear. No rollback is now possible. Even Chiang Kai-shek has given up his dream of returning to the mainland. But containment too has failed. There is no alliance system or common market in East Asia comparable to West Europe.

The most significant manifestation of this failure, aside from Indochina, has been the rise of Japan. As American power is diminishing in East Asia, the Japanese are rapidly expanding their political and military roles. This is coupled with the erosion of the main bond between Japan and the U. S.—trade—manifest in the rising protectionist sentiment within the U. S.

China experts have a regrettable habit of separating China from Vietnam, talking of U. S.-China relations as if they did not have a direct bearing on Indochina. I would like to suggest a way in which they have been connected—by the Chinese. The Chinese have made an approach to America, indirectly by way of Cambodia. To my mind, the most significant manifestation of change in Chinese foreign policy has not been sending ambassadors back to their posts, but the fact that, through their support of Sihanouk, they have offered the Americans a road identical with that offered by the NLF for South Vietnam and the Pathet Lao for Laos.

There are now three proposals: Vietnamese (PRG) aimed at Saigon, Cambodian supported by China, and Pathet Lao. All say the same thing: that a solution is possible through coalition governments. In such governments, the left will acquire important power. They will carry out land reform. But if one reads the political program of Sihanouk's government, or the PRG, or the Pathet Lao, one sees that there would be no total communist takeover, no abolition of private property, no pulling out of the international market. Feudalism and the parasitic aspects of capitalism would be abolished, but socialism not fully introduced. They are saying they will make these countries half-communist, but not more.

The larger communist powers, primarily China, will guarantee this understanding with the U. S., whether in a signed agreement or not. Previously the Chinese did not support the North Vietnamese and the NLF in their call for coalition governments. Yet hardly anyone in the U. S. has seen fit to point out this new Chinese approach. The China "experts" keep on lamenting that the Chinese make no response to the new American initiatives toward them.

There will be a quadrangular situation in Asia among the great powers: China, Japan, Russia, America. That is good. I subscribe to DeGaulle's notion that many big powers are better than two. The bipolar notion (America and Russia) is a failure; worse yet, it is leading to a renewal of the arms race. In that quandrangular situation, the U. S. will have to play a reduced role. The Chinese estimate that U. S. power in East Asia is on a downward course. Only a massive reversal, requiring a huge American military mobilization, could reverse this trend. They recognized the change right after Johnson's October 31, 1968, speech. They showed it by reprinting Nixon's inaugural address in full in *Red Flag*.

It would be better for America to accept the inevitable and jump into the ice-cold water. Such acceptance means more than trivial concessions to China or a change in rhetoric. It means abandoning Saigon and Phnom Penh and Vientiane as bastions of U. S. power. That is the core not just of peace in Vietnam, but of developing viable relations with the People's Republic of China. Getting out of Indochina is the key to a new relationship with China.

VI

EPILOGUE

EARL C. RAVENAL

Beyond 1972:
The Political-Military Gap

"It's *his* doctrine," Henry Kissinger is reported to have said,[1] justifying the president's implementation of the Nixon Doctrine, "and he can damned well do what he wants with it." If this belligerent scrap of sophistry proves one thing, it is that the keys to understanding a policy are not to be found in the text. President Nixon's second State of the World message [2] exemplifies the point. After his first diffident and oblique statement at Guam in July 1969, the president has acquired increasing confidence in the self-canonizing formula, the "Nixon Doctrine," just as staff sycophants have applied it to every American act and intention—to the point where it is difficult to discern what, if anything, it confers on the diverse and sometimes irreconcilable actions that are identified as flowing from it. Under the semantic cover of the Nixon Doctrine, the administration cuts American military strength in Japan and Okinawa, substitutes for it in Vietnam and Korea, maintains it in Europe, and increases it in the Mediterranean.

In particular, the gloss-term "partnership" has been extended over the concept for Asia (self-reliance) as well as the concept for Europe (burden-sharing). But what is evident is

1. Robert Keatley, "Slipping Slopes in Cambodia?" *Wall Street Journal,* January 29, 1971, p. 26.
2. Richard Nixon, *U. S. Foreign Policy for the 1970's (II): Building for Peace,* February 25, 1971.

rather the divergence in the practical treatment of the two areas. In Asia, military equipment and highly technical combat and logistic support are furnished by the U. S., and U. S. conventional forces are not only withdrawn from the theater but deleted from the force structure committed to future Asian contingencies—suggesting recourse, in an extremity, to a nuclear demonstration or strike. In Europe, by contrast, the threat of American troop withdrawal is employed to secure an allied contribution of financial resources and qualitative force improvement, while in the end U. S. forces are guaranteed at their present levels, conventional defense is reaffirmed, and our tactical nuclear weapons, though retained on site, are prudently specified as deterrents to a Soviet initiation of theater nuclear war.

What keys do we have to President Nixon's protean doctrine? It might be useful to look at a policy or doctrine as a conditional prediction of national action. This characterization avoids the nonoperational emphasis on intention as well as the tautological assertion that policy is nothing more than the sum of the outputs themselves and therefore does not reveal itself except in retrospect. It has the further virtue of elevating subpolicy elements (such as resource constraints, institutional bias, and other situational factors) to a consideration that is commensurate with the normally acknowledged, deliberate elements of the policy-formation process. Accordingly, we should disregard even what a policy is *intended* to mean by its authors—since this might be self-contradictory or fictitious—and concentrate on what it *can* mean, in terms of a working model of the active elements that produce national actions. This is not to insist on the special validity of any particular abstract scheme. It is simply to suggest that a serious effort to predict the direction of a nation's responses to future contingencies requires the construction of some model of what produces these responses. In short, it is to attempt to arrive at a conception of "U. S. intentions" such as a possible adversary might view them.

A proper model would be an analytical scheme of the

objective situation that includes the principal operational elements: [3]

1. the logical framework of available (realizable) choices, with their costs, trade-offs, and entailments;

2. the initial policy objects, inherited or preferred—that is, the scope of interests and de facto commitments;

3. the active motivational factors, including personal and institutional propensities, recognitions of constraints, calculations of support, and projective perceptions of results;

4. the constraints, in the form of (a) resource limitations expressed in budgetary stringencies; (b) attitudinal factors such an antitax and anti-defense-spending sentiments that reinforce fiscal stringencies, or antidraft and antimilitary sentiments that force military institutional modifications, or anti-intervention sentiments that bound the strategy horizon; and (c) elements in the international environment, such as large-power or revolutionary resistance, that pose risks at various points in the spectrum of possible actions and produce stalemates and situation denials;

5. the bias of the bureaucratic institutions—the interpretation of constraints; the codification of permissible alternatives and trade-offs; the innovations, accommodations, and compromises;

6. the scenarios that occur—the actualization of contingencies.

Only the resultants of some such scheme and process become the actual choices that are made or the restraints observed. In this way a new pattern of policy outputs and accompanying support structures—including the civil-military relationship—evolves.

At the minimum, the declaratory foreign policy statements of the White House should be read in conjunction with the annual budget statement to Congress by the secretary of defense.[4] Laird's Defense Report, stripped of its heavy overbur-

3. A diagram of the policy process appears in Figure 1 on the following page.
4. Melvin R. Laird, *Defense Report* (before the House Armed Services Committee), March 9, 1971.

Figure 1: MODEL OF THE POLICY PROCESS

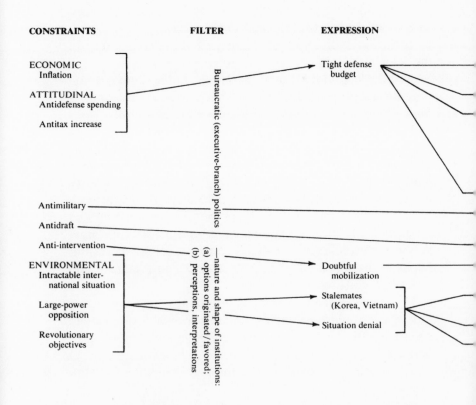

NOTES: 1. The model is
        (*a*) partial: it is primarily a constraint model; it assumes a sub-
            stantive structure of choice, an initial set of policy objects,
            and a direction of preference;
        (*b*) qualitative: it traces the main paths, but has no coefficients
            and no correlation percentages;
        (*c*) qualified: the categories are not blank, but contain indications
            of the nature, or direction, of the effects;
        (*d*) situational: it describes a certain situation, rather than all sit-
            uations in the abstract;
        (*e*) political: it includes some economic terms (e.g., inflation,
            defense spending), but only as they function in the political

218

DIRECT INTERMEDIATE RESULTANTS	TRADE-OFF TERMS	ULTIMATE CONSEQUENCES

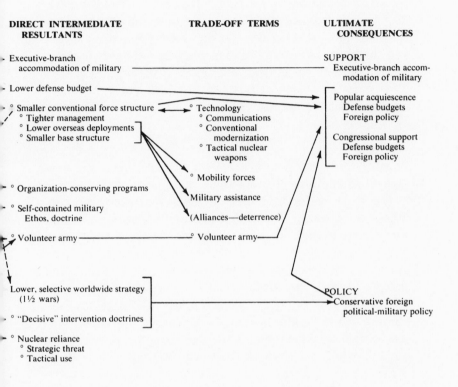

process; the economic terms could be abstracted from this model and in-put to a model of the economy as such;

(f) redundant: some terms are carried forward and appear in two columns (e.g., tactical nuclear weapons as a direct intermediate resultant and a trade-off term; executive-branch accommodation of military as a direct intermediate resultant and an ultimate consequence).

2. The prefixed symbol ° indicates characteristics of the new military structure, whether they are direct intermediate resultants or trade-off terms.

den of merchandising appeal, amplifies the meaning of the State of the World message and contributes clues to the probable implementation of the Nixon Doctrine: (1) the strategic dispositions assumed for planning purposes; (2) the predilections for tactical doctrines; (3) the forces, weapons systems, and conditions of deployability likely to be found in our structure at some future critical time; and (4) the institutional arrangements and planning processes that will shape the advice rendered and the decisions made.

"Stability" For Asia?

A word frequently used in the 1971 State of the World message, that conveniently represents the general thrust of the Nixon Doctrine, is "stability." A moment's reflection establishes that "stability" is a neutral and sophisticated euphemism for "containment." The irony, however, is that "stability" implies a *more* ambitious scope for the application of containment than did previous notions of containment, which more sharply—even if more ideologically—specified its object. The Nixon Doctrine promises the sufferance of change only according to our "understandings"—which are themselves subject to heuristic reinterpretation that feeds progressively on our occasional successes and the acquiescence of our adversaries. Secretary Laird's dual insistence on "vigorous negotiation" supported by "realistic deterrence" [5] reverses the normal process of aggressive gains confirmed by peace settlements, and installs an era of creeping unilateral understandings stabilized by threats of protective retaliation.

There is no doubt that stability implies a continuing attachment to the territorial aspect of the status quo. Our national strategy for Asia is still based on forward defense. This is the operational instruction that our government continues to give its military departments, and toward which our strategies, contingency plans, deployment, forces, and weapons are

5. Ibid., pp. 2, 159.

shaped—and in terms of which "threats" are identified and construed. There is no sign, verbal or tangible, of the relinquishing of interest in the territory of an ally or a buffer state, least of all in the face of pressure or threat. In fact, our forward line of defense in Asia, formerly drawn across four arbitrarily and unstably divided nations, is now drawn across five. And, paradoxically, every situational advantage we seize to get military leverage increases and perpetuates instability, rather than conducing to stability.

The second State of the World message does not yet contain a feasible approach to China.[6] Rather, it expresses an unusually pious invitation to China to accede to an advanced American design for East Asia: a quadrilateral power balance, the "stability" of which is to be insured by the encirclement of China by its three most recent enemies—Russia, the United States, and Japan. The extraordinary piety of this invitation has been widely mistaken for a new liberality of approach. But Chinese accession to this design is to be conditional on its acceptance of President Nixon's vicarious redefinition of China's "legitimate national interests."

There is, for example, the stupefying disjuncture of the discussion of Indochina from the treatment of "the problem of China." Perhaps what is not mentioned is thereby put beyond discussion, and Nixon intends to require the Chinese to take for granted an independent noncommunist South Vietnam and a perpetual American-enforced military standoff throughout Southeast Asia. He also attempts to adjust China's interest in Taiwan, for which he puts forth a conception that is irreconcilable with any position ever taken by the People's Republic of China. In a section that reaffirms our defense commitment to the Republic of China on Taiwan and adumbrates a diplomatic attempt to secure a Two China solution in the United Nations, Nixon postulates: "I do not believe that this honorable and peaceful association need constitute an ob-

6. See Nixon, *Foreign Policy,* pp. 92, 98, 105–109.

stacle to the movement toward normal relations between the United States and the People's Republic of China." It may well be the U. S., not China, that "faces perhaps the most severe problem of all in adjusting her policies to the realities of modern Asia."

Without the complicity of China, which we cannot compel, we and our allies cannot even achieve an untroubled and lasting solution around the periphery of China. We may experiment with limited, almost symbolic, approaches or adopt for a few seasons the transient pose of Two Chinas. But to defend our present basic stance, if seriously tested—diplomatically by other nations or even in belligerent probes by China—would be dangerous and ultimately unproductive. Containment of China, though verbally muted in the second State of the World message, is still the basic condition of the Asian policy of the United States. Talk about "stability" does not change the issues, exorcise the risks and costs, or widen the options. If it fails to come to terms with "the problem of China" by decision, the Nixon administration cannot solve it by transubstantiation.

The Laotian Paradigm

The latest American adventure in Asia, the Laotian invasion, can be taken as a paradigm of the Nixon Doctrine in application. President Nixon, various administration officials, and senior military commanders professed to be heartened at the coming of age of the Army of the Republic of Vietnam (ARVN). But even beyond the shallowness of the penetration, the indecisiveness of the interdiction, and the extent of the casualties, it can be questioned whether the ARVN has acquired fighting capabilities that vindicate the technical goals of Vietnamization. The South Vietnamese offensive was abjectly dependent on continuing U. S. support for logistics, engineering, rear area security, airlift, and above all, close air strikes.

But the ultimate problem does not lie there. The operation, even if it had been successful, was not self-terminating: it did not contain within its purpose or scope the possibility of decisively knocking out the enemy or convincing him to stop. Indeed, the effort contained the principle of its own stultification: the closer we might come to defeating the forces of North Vietnam, the more we threaten and provoke China, which can never accept this result and must move to rectify the situation—this time not necessarily in a wholesale and undifferentiated fashion, but in selective and sufficient ways, either in Laos or in North Vietnam—and so at least enable its ally to redress the balance and stay in the game.

Even an incipient intervention by China would immediately pose starkly for the U. S. the neglected issue of war termination and invoke the ultimate choices: retire from the field; last out an open-ended conventional escalation; or resort to the tactical, demonstrative, or coercive use of nuclear weapons. Studies done at the Pentagon in the late 1960s led to the same conclusion: with conventional arms, we might at great cost prevent the Chinese from a successful military extension beyond their own borders, but once we had engaged them we could not foresee an end to the fighting. It does not matter for this analysis that we may be clever enough to stop short of provoking China's actual intervention. For that is the whole point: we must talk and act as if we are not "threatening" China. This is the obstacle to victory in a peripheral war such as Indochina. The self-limiting—and therefore self-perpetuating—character of this war well illustrates one of the multiple. equivocations in the concept of "limited war": limits of scope or means defy limits of time; we can't keep a war limited and win it.

Vietnamization at its best would give South Vietnam the capacity, with our continuing support and at its heavy expense, to frustrate a revolutionary political or military solution and prolong both the war and the risk of involving its American sponsors in a larger conflict with China. The analogue with the Nixon Doctrine in the large is that the latter promises nothing but implicit involvement in Asia, intermediate objectives that both enlarge and recede with the euphoria of temporary successes, and no acceptable way to terminate a war. The pursuit of "stability" becomes a permanent stabilizing operation and an indefinite postponement of the accommodations of politics and power that might lead to a self-sustaining situation.

One Simultaneous War

In projecting its new military policy, the Nixon administration strains to distinguish it from the policy, strategies, and force structures of its predecessors, which it characterizes:

> A planning goal (never attained) to gain capability for fighting large Asian and European conflicts simultaneously; pursuit of a capability for fighting and training others to fight limited wars and insurgencies; and large but declining foreign and military assistance programs. Significant change in strategy was the shift in emphasis to greater orientation for U. S. toward bearing the principal Free World burden in non-nuclear conflict. . . . In General Purpose Forces, divisions, warships and tactical air squadrons, except fighter-interceptors, increased substantially. Manpower increased by over one million men, due largely to Vietnam. . . . Heavy reliance on use of the draft for conflict, rather than available Reserve forces.[7]

The professed departures of the Nixon administration, as one distills them from Secretary Laird's budget statement for fiscal year 1972, are: (1) a "1½ war" capability, including allied forces, supported by "security assistance," and relying on U. S. reserve units for larger contingencies; and (2) the design of forces for "deterrence" at the relative expense of war-fighting sufficiency.

The detailing of the 1½ war strategy for 1972 confirms an inference that could have been drawn from the prior year's

7. Laird, *Defense Report*, p. 13.

announcement of this new planning base: that the conventional land forces required to defend in either theater would be held in or primarily committed to NATO, and deleted almost entirely from Asia:

> With regard to U. S. force capabilities in Asia, we do not plan for the long term to maintain separate large U. S. ground combat forces specifically oriented just to this theater, but we do intend to maintain strong air, naval and support capabilities. If a large land war involving the United States should occur in Asia, we would, of course, be prepared to mobilize, and would initially use our non-NATO-committed forces as well as portions of those forces based in the U. S. and earmarked for NATO, if required and feasible, and with emphasis on our air and naval capabilities. In the future, we expect the emphasis in Asia more and more to be placed on U. S. support to our allies who themselves provide the required manpower.[8]

Thus, where the prior year's version of the two-directional strategy was unclear in its allocation of ground forces to the two theaters, NATO and Asia, the 1972 statement resolves this ambiguity—and exposes some contradictions: (a) Forward defense is maintained for all allied territory in Asia, but U. S. ground forces are to be almost completely removed from this theater. (b) Quick redeployment is specified, but crippling deficiencies are acknowledged in lift resources. (c) Mobilization of reserves is counted upon, but the units remain undermanned and ill-equipped. (d) Extravagant security assistance is provided, but this involves us more implicitly and postpones the political stabilization we intend.

The conventional forces to implement the 1½ war strategy emerge more clearly as the Department of Defense returns to "baseline" (peacetime) planning. Secretary Laird proposes a ground force, by the end of fiscal year 1972, of 16⅓ active divisions (13⅓ army and 3 marine) and 9 reserve divisions (8 army and 1 marine). Active tactical air wing equivalents are

8. Ibid., p. 77.

in a ratio of 2⅓ for each active land division. (This compares with the baseline program of the Johnson administration: 19⅓ active and 9 reserve divisions, and a tactical air ratio of 2.12.) Withholding 8 active divisions for a NATO contingency and 2⅓ for a minor contingency and other missions leaves 6 divisions available for the early stages of an Asian contingency (compared with the previous administration's 9 divisions)—a reservation of American land forces that has not been considered adequate to the possible demands upon it. And there will probably be further cuts before mid-decade.

This, of course, is precisely the type of allocative dissection that the Nixon administration hopes to avoid with its strategy of 1½ wars and its policy of "realistic deterrence," which frustrate the precise matching of conventional requirements against conventional capabilities. But if one were to make the effort to justify the evolving defense posture, several assumptions might be invoked.

1. The specific deletion of U. S. forces from the Asian defense mission (with their retention primarily for NATO) might imply a reduction of interest or an attenuation of commitment in that area. But speculation in this direction is not encouraged in any official statement of the Nixon administration.

2. Alternatively, estimates of the threat in Asia—not simply the threat of simultaneous conflicts in Europe and Asia—might have been downgraded. One might suspect, sympathetically, that such an assumption underlies the new planning basis. But official statements on this point are sparse, unclear, and contradictory. President Nixon says:

> The situation in Asia differs significantly from that in Europe. The People's Republic of China has substantial military forces. But those forces pose a more limited and less immediate threat in Asia than do the forces of the Soviet Union in Europe.[9]

9. Nixon, *Foreign Policy*, p. 181.

But Secretary Laird mentions only China's difficulty in fighting "on more than one front." [10] Soft impressions of enemy intentions, for a military analyst, are still not a respectable basis for planning forces, and in fact the hard accepted figures on Asian communist capabilities, both conventional and theater nuclear, have edged *upward* since the prior year's Defense Report.[11]

3. Another reconciling assumption would be dependence on strategic mobility. Secretary Laird, while admitting the critical role of sealift to the execution of the new two-directional defense strategy, also admits its critical deficiency: "We face serious sealift problems in executing the rapid deployment concept required under our national strategy in the early stages of a contingency." [12] Troop ships, cargo ships, and tankers directly controlled by the Department of Defense in 1972 will have declined from the level of 1964. Other vessels in the U. S. merchant marine are not reliable because of their normal worldwide dispersal and their inadequate configuration to carry heavy, outsize division equipment. In circumstances where planned U. S. troop deployments will be far less forward than in the concept of his predecessors, Secretary Laird is requesting—not assuredly receiving—sealift resources that would not even be sufficient to implement the second-best rapid deployment plan described by Secretary McNamara in 1968.[13]

4. An innovation in the fiscal year 1972 Defense Report is the clear reliance on reserve forces, rather than the draft, to make good on the deficit of forces that might be occasioned by a large contingency in Asia or a set of simultaneous crises in Europe and Asia:

10. Laird, *Defense Report,* p. 52.
11. Ibid., pp. 48–53.
12. Ibid., p. 99.
13. Robert S. McNamara, Statement before the Senate Armed Services Committee, prepared January 22, 1968, by the Department of Defense, pp. 141–143.

One major step we have taken is our new policy with respect to Reserve Forces. Members of the National Guard and Reserve, instead of draftees, will be the initial and primary source for augmentation of the active forces in any future emergency requiring a rapid and substantial expansion of the active forces.[14]

But the adequacy of this approach is threatened by deficiencies in the manning and equipping of the reserve units. As Secretary Laird explains:

Manning levels will represent a continuing problem as we move toward an all-volunteer force . . . waiting lists for entrance into some Reserve units are declining . . . equipment levels are a current and serious problem for Reserve component readiness. We must insure that the Reserve component units are provided equipment in sufficient quantity, and in combat-serviceable condition, to be effective fighting forces upon mobilization. . . . The overall situation in the Reserve components today is that equipment availability and quality limit combat readiness to levels below those imposed by manpower limitations.[15]

The magnitude of the problem can be measured by Secretary Laird's description of the shortfall of equipment. At the end of 1970 army reserve components had on hand about $1.6 billion out of $6.1 billion needed for mobilization status. Though about $1.3 billion will have been allocated during fiscal years 1970 to 1972, the forces now to be relied upon to take up the slack of the 1½ war strategy will still be vastly under-equipped, and equipment is not a short lead-time category. Even the ten brigades that are "earmarked in our plans for early deployment in the event of a major contingency" are expected to have the minimum 80 percent of their equipment only by the end of 1971. And the rifles and helicopters in the hands of our now-crucial reserves are, on the average, inferior to those we have given the forces of South Vietnam and, in

14. Laird, *Defense Report,* p. 36.
15. Ibid., p. 101.

some cases, South Korea. Air Force Reserve and Air National Guard units, though by their nature in a more active posture, dispose almost uniformly of aircraft of early Korean War vintage—a situation which will only be remedied slowly during the 1972–1976 period.

5. The most critical assumption for the sufficiency of the Nixon administration's Asian strategy is the reliability of foreign military forces. The argument in the secretary's 1972 posture statement for "security assistance" to foreign allies and "friends" is as fervent as the previous year's, and more explicit. Under any label, this policy is not novel, nor is it even a throwback to the Eisenhower years. It has been the policy of every president and secretary of defense since the time of Truman. In addition to Secretary Laird's insistence on the economies of this approach that derive from comparative advantage in the allocation of defensive roles,[16] President Nixon specifies further objectives for the security assistance program: "In some theaters the threshold of involvement will be raised and in some instances involvement will be much more unlikely." [17] This triple rationale is precisely that of Secretary Clifford in expounding military assistance in his Memorandum to the President of January 1969.

There are, however, some novelties in the functions of American allies and arms under the Nixon Doctrine. One is the complete dependence of the Doctrine on the hope that military assistance will fill the gap between continued policy objectives and declining U. S. general purpose force capabilities. (The obverse of this is the greater eagerness to *count* allied forces as part of a "Total Force" concept.) Pentagon officials of the preceding administration were more skeptical, even while rehearsing the traditional dogmas, and toward the end were inclined to consider reducing the reach of U. S. commitments rather than invest even more immodestly in the military forces of allied governments.

16. Ibid., p. 34
17. Nixon, *Foreign Policy,* p. 14.

A second departure is the indication that the Nixon administration has finally begun to give operational significance to
the concept of comparative advantage, by planning to implement the cost-effective specialization of the roles of U. S. and
allied forces. Secretary Laird makes several exemplary statements of this purpose:

> Military manpower is more costly for the U. S. than for any
> of our allies . . . adjustments should be made in the balance
> of U. S. and allied contributions to our combined capabilities
> to better use the advantages of each country as we move to-
> ward more self-reliant allied capabilities.[18]

Later he projects the "appropriate restructuring of our own
forces with the objective of complementing allied capabilities
more effectively" [19]—a shorthand reference to changing the
traditional overall balance of the units in our own force structure to optimize their integration with the defective force
structure of a foreign forward defense country.

The third novelty is the Nixon administration's success in
reversing the declining appropriations for security assistance.
During the budget years controlled by the Johnson administration, from 1965 through 1970, the average annual value of
total U. S. defense assistance and subsidized arms traffic to its
allies and friends was slightly less than $5 billion.[20] During
the first Nixon budget year, 1971, these values attained $6.8
billion; and the amount for fiscal year 1972 will probably
have totaled over $7 billion by the end of that year. Accord-
ing to this more inclusive accounting, the United States will
have spent, in more than two decades, perhaps $40–50 billion
to shore up East Asian client governments.

Has this assistance brought closer the common goals of a

18. Ibid., p. 78.
19. Ibid., p. 84.
20. This accounting relies on the inclusive format used by Under Secretary
of State John N. Irwin II in his presentation to the Subcommittee on
Economy in Government of the Joint Economic Committee of the Congress,
February 2, 1971 (*The Department of State Bulletin,* February 22, 1971, p.
226).

succession of presidents, to raise the threshold and lower the probability of involvement? On the contrary, our amplified provision of security assistance, coupled with our evolving assumption of a complementary role of support, in a context of unrelieved forward defense of the territorial integrity of our client states, is likely to perpetuate conflict and involve us in a contingency from the earliest moment, not simply at such later time as it began to appear that our military client could not "hack it." Nixon admits: "No President can guarantee that future conflicts will never involve American personnel." [21] And Laird recognizes: "There may be situations where only U. S. capabilities would provide the flexibility of action which may be necessary in the future.[22]

If the Nixon program guarantees anything, it is that a future Asian crisis would be faced in an atmosphere of desperate improvisation. And should allied forces be threatened with collapse, U. S. decision-makers, facing the agonizing questions of deployment and mobilization, and considering respectfully the necessary reservations for NATO and other requirements, would be commensurately tempted to rise to nuclear threats, demonstrations, or strikes.

Deterrence Revisited

The fiscal year 1972 defense concept to implement the Nixon Doctrine is branded "realistic deterrence." We should resist an initial impulse to call this a mere slogan; the term is pregnant with possible meaning. The strategists of the Nixon administration set out to remedy a perceived defect in the planning of their predecessors: "This was the failure to correlate closely and fully military strategy, national security strategy, and foreign policy." [23] This is a curious charge for them to level, for the effect of "deterrence" is to confirm the severence of the

21. Nixon, *Foreign Policy*, p. 14.
22. Laird, *Defense Report*, p. 107.
23. Ibid., p. 12.

link between (a) the force requirements generated by our continuing commitments in all theaters, and (b) the force structure, which has already, in response to institutional demands, popular pressures, and budgetary convenience, begun to take its own shape.

The concept of deterrence, to be more than idly asserted, must be distinguishable from the concept of defense. To the extent that it is proposed, it embodies two characteristic notions: (1) that the forces, weapons, and tactical doctrines are to be offensive, and are only coincidentally useful for defense; and (2) that even this offensive complex is to be optimized for its destructive and psychologically preemptive features, and is only coincidentally useful for defeating an enemy's forces or terminating a war. To the extent that one is committed to deterrence, then, one hopes to obviate not only the need for adequate defensive force, but even the question of its relevance. To be fair to Secretary Laird, it is necessary to point out that he also professes to seek "an adequate warfighting capability, both in limited nuclear and conventional options." [24] But the direction of the force structure is more important—and more revealing—than the direction of the rhetoric; and we have reviewed the force deficiencies that impair the exercise of the conventional defense option.

Deterrence generically promises escalatory initiative, and the modern variant of deterrence suggests the earlier introduction of nuclear weapons in the scale of escalation. But President Nixon rejects a return to the simplistic "massive retaliation" of the 1950s, which could "pose an agonizing choice between paralysis and holocaust." [25] Instead, he adheres to a doctrine which he tendentiously calls *"truly* flexible response." [26] The departure from the flexible response of the 1960s is that we will not have the same levels of appropriate response as before. Criteria for the level and the range of

24. Ibid., p. 18.
25. Nixon, *Foreign Policy*, p. 5.
26. Ibid., p. 19. Italics added.

possible—and permissible—response have been greatly affected by technology and disillusion with the (supposed) application of simply countervailing force throughout the Vietnam war. The new direction is foreshadowed in Nixon's statement:

> . . . having a full range of options does not mean that we will necessarily limit our response to the level or intensity chosen by an enemy. Potential enemies must know that we will respond to whatever degree is required to protect our interests. They must also know that they will only worsen their situation by escalating the level of violence.[27]

This statement not only promises that we will take the lead in initiating, if necessary, an advance to a higher level of violence; it also gives some further clue to what a mating of "realistic deterrence" with "truly flexible response" might mean in practice. If even *"having* a full range of options," including a purportedly viable conventional option, does not insure keeping within the bounds of a limited and sufficient response, then certainly *not* having this range of options would force us to threaten to transcend this limitation. This deduction has particular implications for Asia, which are exemplified in the divergent treatment of NATO and Asia under the Nixon Doctrine. In NATO, the conventional option has been extended; U. S. combat forces will not be withdrawn until they are replaced with equivalent allied conventional strength, qualitative or quantitative. In Asia, however, the progressive withdrawal of American ground forces is to be compensated by the lightly tested and prayerful substitution of indigenous forces, and by the promise of rapid reintroduction of U. S. troops, which would have to come from our strategic reserves and even from those forces "earmarked for NATO." "Should deterrence fail" in Asia, then the consequences could be quite open-ended.

Speculation as to the possible range of consequences must take account of a perceptible reappraisal of the utility of nu-

27. Ibid., p. 179.

clear weapons in theater wars. The discussion of theater nuclear weapons in the fiscal year 1972 Defense Report is more extensive and more serious than in recent years:

> In considering theater nuclear war, i.e., enemy use of nuclear weapons overseas without a direct attack on the U. S., we must recognize both the utility of all weapons systems in contributing to deterrence including the capabilities of our allies, and the limitations that influence the use of systems designed for one level of warfare in another level . . .
>
> By the same token, but even more so, our theater and tactical nuclear weapons add to the realism of deterrence of theater conventional wars in Europe and Asia; the Soviets and Chinese Communists cannot be sure that major conventional aggression would not be met with the tactical use of nuclear weapons.
>
> . . . We must plan our theater nuclear weapon posture and relate it to our conventional posture in such a way that we have a realistic option in the theater without having to rely solely on strategic nuclear weapons. In other words, we plan to maintain tactical nuclear capabilities that contribute to realistic deterrence while allowing for maximum flexibility of response in every major contingency we plan for should deterrence fail.
>
> . . . research and development and weapon improvement programs are planned in this area . . . with such programs, we believe that we can retain or improve the essential contribution our theater nuclear forces make to our deterrent posture.[28]

The spectrum of possible nuclear escalation also now includes the selective use of strategic nuclear weapons to achieve limited coercive or destructive purposes. As President Nixon puts it, discussing strategic nuclear forces:

> We must insure that we have the forces and procedures that provide us with alternatives appropriate to the nature and level of the provocation. This means having the plans and

28. Laird, *Defense Report*, pp. 75–76.

command and control capabilities necessary to enable us to select and carry out the appropriate response without necessarily having to resort to mass destruction.[29]

Aside from such indications of interest—and the rigid logic of the alternatives—there is a mixed collection of evidence for the continuing, and perhaps increasing, viability of the nuclear option for theater contingencies. (1) There has been no significant net change in the number and forward deployment of tactical nuclear weapons in Europe or East Asia. (2) Deployment, procurement, and development of new tactical nuclear systems continues; and the salient feature of the three new systems mentioned by Secretary Laird—WALLEYE, LANCE, and an "Improved 155mm Projectile" [30]—is increased accuracy. (3) The ROAD concept of army force organization, which replaced the exclusively nuclear "Pentomic" configuration in the early 1960s, does not preclude rapid posturing for tactical nuclear war. (4) There has lately been a quickened advocacy of nuclear reliance in the public writings of middle-grade military officers, journalist-strategists, and defense academics. (5) There is now strengthened institutional support for nuclear alternatives within the office of the secretary of defense—notably among the International Security Affairs staff—that reinforces the persistent nuclear orientation of the Joint Chiefs of Staff and such significant unified commands as CINCPAC.

Further developments of theater nuclear weaponry could take several forms, not necessarily exclusive: (1) refinement of strictly tactical nuclear weapons and the accompanying doctrine for their employment; (2) exploitation of the cost-effective use of strategic-sized nuclear weapons in the theaters—a "terrain fire" or "blanket fire" approach; (3) elaboration of Nixon's ominous proposal of a more selective use of truly strategic weapons.

29. Nixon, *Foreign Policy*, p. 173.
30. Laird, *Defense Report*, p. 161.

If this necessarily speculative account construes the strategic direction of the Nixon administration with even a modicum of correctness, there is danger in the hybridization of "realistic deterrence" with "truly flexible response." One might concede that the requisite subtlety and intensity of intellect to cope with the expanded range of options, scenarios, and countermoves is amply provided by the staff of the National Security Council. But it is still respectable to reaffirm the stubborn wisdom of the counter-nuclear thinkers of the 1950s and 1960s: that sophisticated notions of the selective and intermediate utility of nuclear weapons bridge a chasm, and thus threaten the safety of all.

The Cult of Support

A foreign policy cannot even be defined without considering the sources of its support. "Support" is a complex of relationships, (a) between the executive branch and the public, the legislature, and certain interested groups, and (b) within the institutions of the executive branch itself. The first set of relationships functions as constraints; the second acts to filter, bias, and shape proposals and programs.

The Nixon administration evidently hopes to carry on its foreign strategy even in the face of adverse opinion readings. And yet the 1971 State of the World message is extraordinarily self-conscious about public support. The contradiction is resolved by noting that its strategy requires—in fact, implies— not active support, but passive acquiescence. For such a cool equilibration of power, neutral exercise of control, and intricate apportionment of roles within our alliances, warm and positive domestic support might even be an embarrassment. President Nixon defines the quality of the support he seeks:

> We must convincingly demonstrate the relationship between our specific actions and our basic purposes. In turn, the leadership can ask the American people for some degree of trust, and for acknowledgement of the complexities of foreign pol-

icy. This does not mean a moratorium on criticism. It means listening to the rationale for specific actions and distinguishing attacks on the broad policy itself from attacks on tactical judgments.[31]

This is a prescription for anesthetizing political dissent and attaining the requisite condition of apathy, bemusement, and deference that sums up to acquiescence.

The concomitant strategy toward the legislative branch would be pacification, in which the legislature could be won by superficial and subtle means of confidence and co-optation. The pattern could include the acceptance of the outlines of congressional resolutions limiting foreign policy and military maneuver; the thin intrusion of a semantic wedge; and the widening of this wedge through subsequent actions. A consultative oligarchy of legislators could be admitted to a sharing of intelligence and a complicity in a basically executive determination of policy.

The military exponents of executive policy are extended the promise of a revitalized professionalism of the Services, a strong "participatory" share in the elaboration of strategy, the determination of procurement and resource allocation, and the prospect of organization-enhancing weapons systems subjected to less stringent justification. Quite naturally, the reaction of the Services to a new national security policy is to accommodate to it by gravitating to where the "action" is—as they all adapted to the unconventional warfare vogue of the 1960s (even the navy was operating in commando units far behind enemy lines). The Services are again competing innovatively, this time to adapt their traditional arms to the aseptic connotations of the Nixon Doctrine. The navy—so far the principal beneficiary—promotes its normal "over-the-horizon" posture (the presumably nonprovocative, standoff readiness to deliver overwhelming force) and its comprehensive "blue-water" strategy (the quiet worldwide reach). The air force insists, characteristically, on the centrality of strategic

31. Nixon, *Foreign Policy*, p. 21.

attack (the attempted destruction of the enemy's will). The army abstracts from its role of closing with the enemy and furthers a new mythology of remote engagement (the automated electronic battlefield and the prompt, precise, lethal reaction).

Conclusion: A Byzantine Age?

Existing pressures and constraints may produce considerable displacement and accommodation of institutions and strategies—without also producing constructive and comprehensible foreign and military policies. There is likely to be a more complaisant arrangement with the military within the national security departments of the executive branch; a tighter, more self-contained military establishment, perhaps better managed, certainly more technologically formidable, and most likely manned by volunteers. There probably will be— particularly for Asia—a more selective strategy of intervention; a more skeletal overseas presence; a large-scale program of force-substitution that relies on allied contributions and U. S. arms transfers and support. This dispensation will probably achieve its appropriate level of popular and congressional acquiescence. On the other hand, the same logic and the same compulsions might bring about nuclear threats, decisive interventions, and remote methods of destruction that obviate human involvement and diffuse moral considerations.

In larger terms, the Nixon Doctrine—the Nixon era itself —can be seen as signaling the beginning of a long secular transit for America. One can sense the emergence of the features of such a mature state as Byzantium—policing a more consolidated empire; exercising a more sophisticated blend of diplomacy and war, manipulation and coercion; deploying more parsimoniously its technically virtuose weapons and mercenary armies; dispensing internal welfare and resting content with a more settled mercantilism; superimposing self-centered executive institutions on a quiescent and deferent political base.

Perhaps one should not overextend the parallel. But the historical analogy also suggests historical choices. The coming age could be neo-imperial, or it could be post-imperial. And the transition could be a grudging, baleful retreat; or it could be a tolerant concession to the condition of America's prospective long haul: the abandonment of the principle that this nation has a privileged purpose that it must impress on the rest of the world.

Index

Date Due